WALKS

IN THE

Lake District

Vivienne Crow

Questa

© Vivienne Crow, 2011

ISBN 978-1-898808-37-4

Maps:

The maps accompanying the walks in this book are purely diagrammatic. The maps for Walks 5, 13, 16, 17 and 18 are based on Ordnance Survey mapping, and are reproduced by permission of Ordnance Suvey on behalf of HMSO © Crown Copyright, 2011. All rights reserved. Ordnance Survey Licence number 100043743. All the remaining maps are based on maps produced by Harvey Maps (Licence No. 93001 © Harvey Map Services Ltd.)

NOTE

No attempt has been made to grade the walks in this book, as this is too subjective. Use the information about distance and height gain to calculate how long the walk will take.

Published by
Questa Publishing Limited,
Bamber Bridge, Lancashire PR5 8LA
www.questapublishing.co.uk

Contents

Introduction	6
Northern Lake District	
1. Sale Fell	12
2. Glenderaterra Valley	15
3. Souther Fell	20
4. Graystones and Broom Fell	23
5. High Pike	27
Eastern Lake District	
6. Gowbarrow and Aira Force	32
7. Red Tarn	36
8. Wansfell ridge from Kirkstone Pass	41
9. Place Fell from Howtown	45
Southern Lake District	
10. Gummer's How	51
11. Grizedale Forest and Hawkshead	53
12. Hawkshead to Near Sawrey via Latterbarrow	58
13. Tarn Hows and Monk Coniston	62
14. Whitbarrow	67
15. Wallowbarrow	72
16. Devoke Water	76
Western Lake District	
17. Around Gosforth	81
18. Loweswater Corpse Road	85
19. Buttermere	89
20. Rannerdale Knotts	93
21. Around Mellbreak	97
22. Eskdale Moor	100
23. Haystacks	104

Short Walks

Central Lake District
24. Castle Crag   107
25. Above Thirlmere   111
26. Alcock Tarn   115
27. Dock Tarn and Great Crag   119
28. Taylorgill Force and Styhead Tarn   123
29. Lingmoor Fell and Side Pike   127
30. Seat Sandal   131

IN THE LAKE DISTRICT

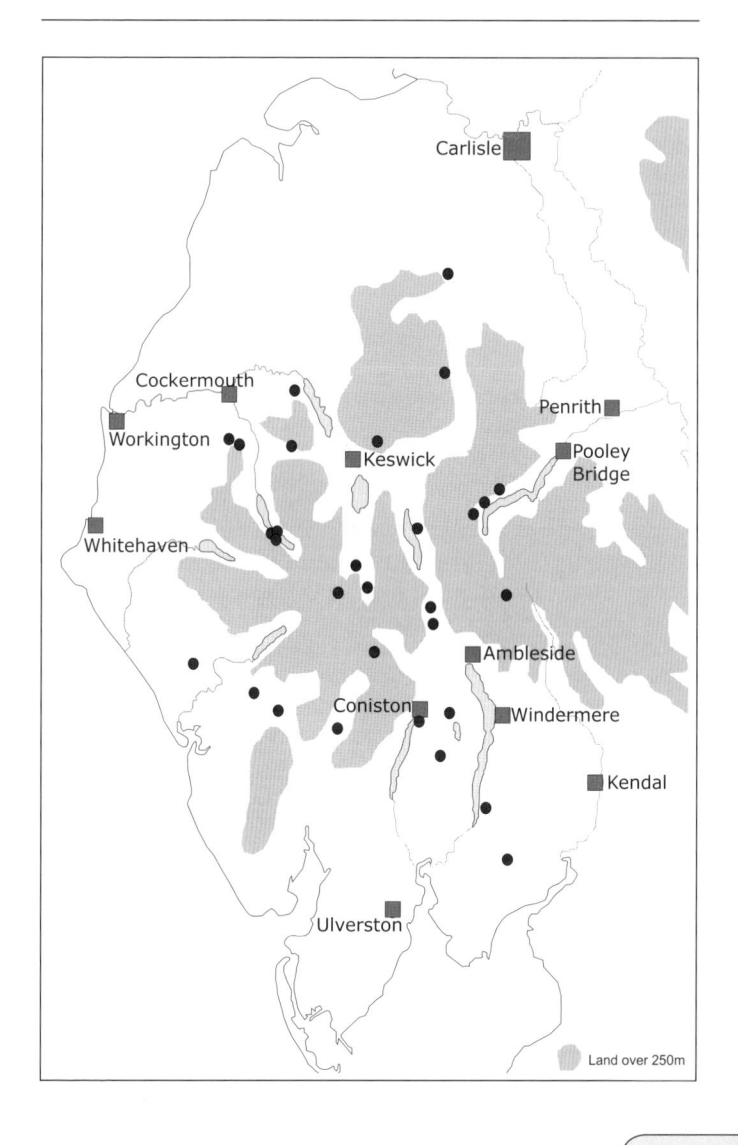

INTRODUCTION

You'd think from glancing through the pages of the dozens and dozens of Lake District guides filling bookshop shelves that walkers have to hike for 10 or 12 miles on the high fells to appreciate the beauty of the National Park, but that couldn't be further from the truth; short routes give you the opportunity to take your time and truly savour what this mountainous corner of England has to offer.

And it has much to offer – as writers and artists have been telling us for centuries. The Romantic poets, most notably, William Wordsworth wrote stanza upon stanza about the grandeur of the mountains, the lake, the daffodils... Artists such as Turner tried to capture the moods of this dramatic landscape on canvas. Today, guidebook writers, photographers and TV presenters continue this tradition of waxing lyrical about the Lake District.

As you walk the routes in this book, you too will understand the reason for this endless enthusiasm – as you round a crag and are stopped in your tracks by a new and dramatic view; as you walk through forests and catch tantalising glimpses, through the trees, of a glittering lake far below. Who can fail to be moved by the sight of sun beams breaking through a moody sky, throwing light and colour on to the rocky fellside? Whose heart is not uplifted by the sight of craggy, snow-covered summits under a sparkling blue sky? And, just when you thought you knew the Lake District and were getting used to its nuances, you will catch a familiar view in a new light or in different weather conditions and understand why this magnificent place continues to capture the imagination.

Like many mountain landscapes, the Lake District is the result of the complex interplay of bedrock, plate movements, processes such as glaciation and then man's intervention. In the simplest terms, it is a massive volcanic dome fissured by tectonic forces and then sculpted by huge rivers of ice to create a spray of valleys and dividing mountain ranges radiating from a central hub – often likened to the spokes on a wheel. Most notably, it was the last glacial period, which ended about

IN THE LAKE DISTRICT

10,000 years ago, that carved and sculpted the land into what we know and love today. The glaciers gouged out deep, u-shaped valleys and created arêtes, waterfalls in hanging valleys and long, narrow lakes held back by piles of clay and stone abandoned by the retreating ice. High in the mountains, the ice plucked out corries, which are now home to smaller bodies of water known as tarns.

The retreating ice sheets left a barren landscape that was slowly colonised by hardy plants such as juniper, mosses and grasses. The area's natural vegetation cover would have become established only a few thousand years ago, and if it hadn't been for man's intervention, that is probably what you would see in much of Cumbria today: the valley bottoms would be impenetrable swamps dotted with alder and dense sedges; there would be oak and elm forest on the lower fells; and then pine and birch woodland up to an altitude of about 600m (2,000ft). It would be a mass of trees with just the rocky tops poking through the woods. Instead, largely because of woodland clearance and grazing, we see exposed rocky slopes and expansive moor and pasture, all partitioned by drystone walls that snake up and down the fells.

Humankind has been leaving its mark on the Lake District landscape since Neolithic times when early quarrymen first braved the steep, rugged slopes of Langdale's Pike o' Stickle to search for volcanic rock to use in axe heads, which were subsequently traded throughout the country. Gazing at those seemingly perfect fells from the road, it is hard to believe that, for millennia, people have lived and worked here, often exploiting the natural resources and frequently leaving indelible scars behind.

The second millennium BC heralded the start of the Bronze Age and the creation of some of the county's most long-lasting and enigmatic remains – stone circles such as mysterious Castlerigg or the scattered cairns and settlements near Devoke Water. Iron Age peoples then brought their advanced farming techniques and their Celtic language, the remains of which are still evident in the names of the county's topographical features today – 'blain' meaning summit, for example, gives rise to 'blen' as in Blencathra; and 'creic' becomes crag.

Short Walks

The next group of 'off-comers' were the Romans, who arrived in Britain in AD43. Although this far north-western outpost of the empire was purely a military zone to them, and Cumbria lacks the villas and markets found elsewhere in England, there is plenty of evidence of Roman roads, forts and other defensive structures throughout the Lake District. Their departure, in the fifth century, marks the start of the Dark Ages, a period of few historical documents and little archaeological evidence, when fact and fiction become intertwined and semi-mythological figures such as King Arthur and Urien of Rheged, a Celtic kingdom covering much of modern-day Cumbria, appear.

As Celtic power declined, the Anglo-Saxons began to control much of lowland Cumbria and the pastoralist Norsemen began settling in the uplands. All left their calling cards in terms of place names, but it is the Norse words that stand out – words such as fell, from the word 'fjell', or mountain in modern Norwegian. The Norse word for waterfall is 'foss', which becomes 'force' in the Lake District; 'tjorn' becomes tarn; 'dalr' becomes dale; and 'bekkr' beck.

The last 1,000 years or so have been a period of great change and, sometimes, bloodshed in the region. The border wars created much instability, fear and insecurity, which is reflected in the architecture of the era. The wealthy families built themselves stout, sturdy pele towers to which they would retreat in the event of attack. Many have survived, such as Kentmere Hall and Muncaster Castle. Meanwhile, powerful monastic houses, most notably the Furness Cistercians, realised wealth could be accrued from the area's natural resources. They began to acquire huge tracts of land for farming sheep – mostly for the wool trade – and for coppicing – for timber and for charcoal destined for the growing number of iron smelting bloomeries. Mining, quarrying and other industries have continued to play a major role in shaping the Lake District ever since. In the 16th century, for example, there was an influx of German miners who tore into the fells around Keswick and Coniston, in particular, digging deep for copper, lead, silver and even gold. The coming of the railways, in the 19th century, then acted as a catalyst for industrial development on an even larger scale.

IN THE LAKE DISTRICT

Despite man's far-reaching influences, Mother Nature still manages to make her presence felt. The fell-tops may seem to be covered in nothing but rock with occasional heathers, bilberry, lichen and mosses, but there are wildflowers too – one can see wood anemone, asphodels, red campion, lady's mantle, bog myrtle, spotted orchids, stonecrop, saw-worth and thrift. Examples of arctic-alpine flora such as bright blue Alpine gentia, roseroot, mountain sorrel and the dainty purple saxifrage still bloom in secluded mountain locations.

In terms of birdlife, the fells are home all year round to ravens, buzzards, peregrines and, in the eastern fells, England's last surviving golden eagle. Red kites were recently released in Grizedale Forest and are expected to range throughout the Lake District in the coming years. Spring migrants include the wheatear and ring ouzel (mountain blackbird). Lower down, in the spring, you'll encounter a range of migratory species, including redstart, pied flycatcher, wood warbler and tree pipit among the year-round residents such as chaffinch, green and great-spotted woodpeckers, nuthatch and sparrowhawk. On the lakes themselves, you can find good numbers of waterfowl, goosander, goldeneye and tufted duck, while rivers and streams are home to dippers, grey wagtails and common sandpipers. A pair of ospreys recently made the Lake District their summer home, returning from wintering in Africa to their nest in Dodd Wood on the shores of Bassenthwaite Lake every April.

Mammals of the high fells include foxes, hares and stoats. Herds of red deer can also be seen above the tree line, especially in the eastern fells. The woods, meanwhile, are home to badgers, roe deer, voles, shrews, the occasional otter and, of course, red squirrels. There have even been some sightings of pine marten in Grizedale and Ennerdale in recent years.

There are some interesting inhabitants to be found in Cumbria's lakes and becks too. The Lake District is the southern limit of the Arctic char, a slender fish that has been here since the last ice sheets disappeared; and vendace, found in Bassenthwaite Lake and Derwent Water, is one of only three freshwater white fish native to Britain.

SHORT WALKS

The Walks

The walks in this book have been divided into five geographical areas: Northern Lake District, Eastern Lake District, Southern Lake District, Western Lake District and Central Lake District. They cover a wide variety of terrain and include lakeside paths, farmland, lowland bridleways, rocky tracks and open moorland. No attempt has been made to grade the walks, as this is too subjective, but, within each of the five areas, they are listed roughly in ascending order of difficulty. Readers should use the information about distance and height gain to calculate how long the walk will take. They differ in length from 2.7km (1¾ miles) to 11.3km (7 miles). Height gain can be anything from 93m (305ft) to 697m (2,286ft), although most are in the region of about 250-400m (820-1,312ft).

A number of low-lying felltops are visited, including Sale Fell (Walk 1), Souther Fell (Walk 3), Gowbarrow (Walk 6) Gummer's How (Walk 10), Latterbarrow (Walk 12), Whitbarrow (Walk 14), Wallowbarrow (Walk 15), Rannerdale Knotts (Walk 20) and Castle Crag (Walk 24), where the emphasis is on fantastic views and reasonably easy walking. Place Fell (Walk 9), Haystacks (Walk 23), Lingmoor Fell (Walk 29) and Seat Sandal (Walk 30), on the other hand, are slightly more strenuous and involve steeper, sometimes rocky ground. For a medium amount of effort, High Pike (Walk 5), Wallowbarrow (Walk 15), Devoke Water (Walk 16), the circuit of Mellbreak (Walk 21) and Eskdale Moor (Walk 22) provide a sense of remoteness that is typical of the fringes of the National Park. But don't expect to have the classic routes such as Buttermere (Walk 19) and Castle Crag (Walk 24) to yourself.

Walks 7, 26 and 27 climb specifically to visit a few of the Lake District's most exquisite tarns – in this case, Red Tarn, Alcock Tarn and Dock Tarn respectively – but most of the other routes in the book also pass some beautifully located bodies of water. Waterfalls too can be seen, most notably on walk six, which passes under the fine spray of Aira Force, and Walk 28, which scrambles alongside Taylorgill Force before continuing on to Styhead Tarn.

Each of the five areas has its own character. In the north are some of the

IN THE LAKE DISTRICT

oldest mountains in the world, composed of Skiddaw slates laid down more than 450 million years ago. Hardened and compressed on the sea bed, these give us smooth, rounded, often grassy fells such as High Pike.

Further south, the rough, angular, craggy landscape is attributed to the Borrowdale volcanic series, made up of hardened lava and ash, the result of a cataclysmic volcanic episode. Today, these rocks form the heart of the Lake District – extending from Wasdale in the west to High Street and Haweswater in the east, taking in the mighty Scafell and Helvellyn ranges along the way.

A thin band of limestone then occurs, separating the volcanics from the softer, sedimentary rocks of the far south of the county, known as the Silurian series. Not unlike the rocks of the northern Lakes, but much younger, these slates, siltstones and sandstones were formed in the sea about 420 million years ago. They have created a belt of relatively low-lying, rolling hills around Windermere and Kendal.

Short Walks

1
Sale Fell

Start/Finish: Roadside parking 200 metres north-east of St Margaret's Church, near Wythop Mill (NY191302)
Distance: 6.1km (3¾ miles)
Height gain: 308m (1,010ft)
Type of walk: Grassy fell; forest tracks and trails
Refreshments: Pheasant Inn, Bassenthwaite

Sale Fell is a lovely little grassy hill close to the north-western tip of Bassenthwaite Lake. The top is a great place to linger with a picnic, particularly on a warm summer's evening when you can watch the sun starting to set over the west coast and then enjoy the warm, pink glow it casts on mighty Skiddaw. There is a short climb onto the 359m summit, but it isn't difficult; the return is via pleasant forest tracks and paths in Wythop Wood.

FROM THE PARKING AREA, CROSS THE ROAD to go through the gate towards Kelswick and up the track. A little way after passing a bench and going through a gap in a drystone wall, the pleasant track starts to swing right. You soon encounter a drystone wall to your right.

Just before the path starts descending, turn left along a grassy path heading straight up the open fellside. In about 60 metres, at the first fork in the path, bear right to ascend the southern edge of the fell with views across to Lord's Seat and Broom Fell. Ignoring a faint path heading downhill to the right, you continue uphill, soon catching your first sighting of Skiddaw to the east.

IN THE LAKE DISTRICT

The view to the NW is opening out too – with the perfect bump of Criffel standing out clearly as you look across the Solway to the coast of Dumfries & Galloway. You soon join up with a path coming in from the left and, in another 50 metres, bear left at another fork. After a few more minutes of easy ascent, you reach the cairn-topped summit of Sale Fell.

Head ESE from the summit cairn to pass through a gate in a wall (hidden from view from the top). Ignoring the faint path off to the left, walk along the wide track to a gap in what is left of a tumbledown wall. Again ignoring a path off to the left, aim for the large cairn on the hillside ahead (SE). Beyond the cairn, swing left (E) to meet up with another path coming in from the left. Ignoring a path off to the right, climb on to a short but delightful, grassy ridge with the massive bulk of Skiddaw dominating the view ahead. Bassenthwaite Lake becomes visible as you reach the highest point of the ridge – as does Keswick to the SE. When you reach the edge of the forest, turn right along a grassy path heading downhill through the bracken. There is a short section of exposed rock as you skirt an area of oak trees.

Much of the Lake District was once covered in oaks like these – as well as birch and pine. Most of the trees were felled to use as wood in the smelting industry, to make bobbins for the textile industry and to allow for grazing. Dense conifer plantations – like the one you are about to enter – were planted during the early part of the 20th century. The Forestry Commission's first planting in the Lake District was at Hospital Plantation, close to the head of Whinlatter Pass, in 1919.

Dropping on to a wide track, turn left. Enter the forest via a gate and you soon join a clear forest track at a hairpin bend. Bear right here, heading downhill. At the next hairpin bend, follow the track round to the right, still heading downhill – do not be tempted by the track off to

Short Walks

Dubwath

Bassenthwaite Lake

Pheasant Inn

START

Sale Fell

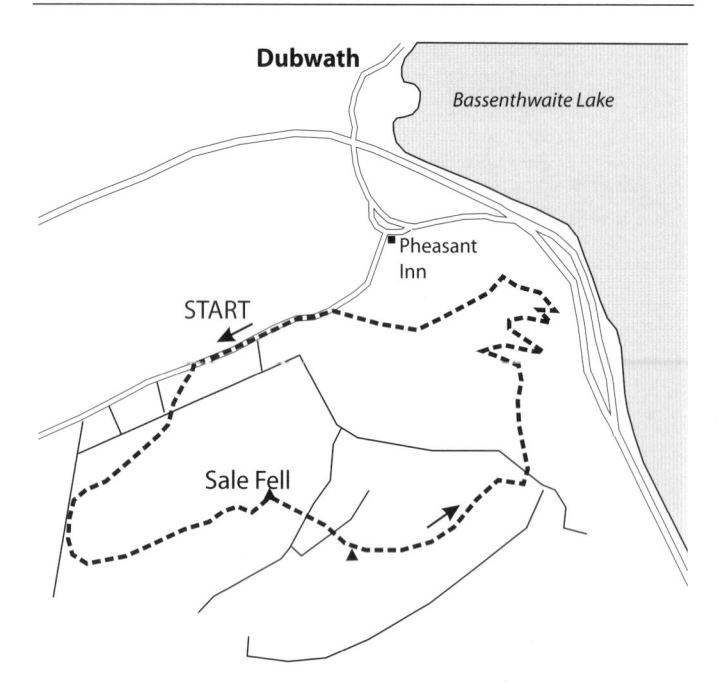

the left. The track zigzags its way down the hillside to a T-junction. Turn left here on to a wide, gravel track.

These woods used to be home to the Lake District's famous **ospreys**, but the couple moved nest – to Dodd Wood on the opposite side of Bassenthwaite Lake – in 2008. These magnificent fish-eating birds of prey returned to Cumbria in 2001 after a 150-year absence and now look set to stay.

The Forestry Commission and Lake District National Park Authority spent years trying to encourage ospreys back to Cumbria after they were persecuted to extinction in the UK by the early part of the 20th century. They built tree-top platforms for the birds, and, finally a passing pair took a fancy to one of these 'nests' and decided to set up home.

IN THE LAKE DISTRICT

They spend the summer in the county, arriving in April and returning to Africa in September, having reared a small family of two or three chicks. A viewing area has been set up in Dodd Wood and volunteers there help visitors spot the birds through powerful binoculars. Watching them fish is quite a sight!

> Just before you reach some buildings, the track bends sharp right. As it does so, take the less distinct path off to the left. Continue straight ahead through the tall conifer trees until you reach the road. Now turn left and the parking area is about 0.5km ahead. ◆

DAFFODILS

Thanks to Wordsworth, daffodils will forever be associated with the Lake District. However, not all of those pretty yellow flowers that you see in the National Park every spring are of the wild variety about which the poet famously waxed so lyrical.

The native Narcissus pseudonarcissus *is a more delicate and graceful plant than its cultivated cousin. It can be identified by its pale yellow outer petals surrounding a golden-yellow trumpet. Its strap-like, upright, grey-green leaves are also distinctive.*

Wild daffodils are generally found on moist banks in open oak or ash woods. Cultivated daffodils, on the other hand, are twice as big as the wild variety and considerably more hardy, having been raised to survive in colder conditions.

Short Walks

2

GLENDERATERRA VALLEY

Start/Finish: Car park just beyond the Blencathra Centre, at the end of Blease Road near Threlkeld (NY302256)
Distance: 9.3km (5¾ miles)
Height gain: 369m (1,210ft)
Type of walk: Mostly good tracks; some farm paths
Refreshments: Salutation Inn and the Horse and Farrier, both in Threlkeld

The Glenderaterra Beck has carved out a narrow, steep-sided valley between Lonscale Fell and Blease Fell, the grassy, western edge of Blencathra. With tracks on both sides of the valley and a car park at almost 300m above sea level, it's easy to access this relatively quiet area of the Lakes. The walk heads up the eastern side of the valley and then returns via the western side. The tracks make for good walking, particularly on the return when you climb to almost 430m with dramatic drops into the valley bottom far below. The final part of the walk takes the walker on to the northern edge of Latrigg, recrosses the Glenderaterra in a pretty woodland setting and then climbs back up to the car park via farm paths and tracks.

FOLLOW THE ROUGH TRACK AWAY FROM THE CAR PARK (WNW). It climbs gently until you get your first uninterrupted view of the steep slopes of Lonscale Fell on the other side of the valley. You can now see straight up the Glenderaterra Beck too. The fell dominating the view beyond the head of the valley is Great Calva. As you make your way up the valley, you can see evidence of

IN THE LAKE DISTRICT

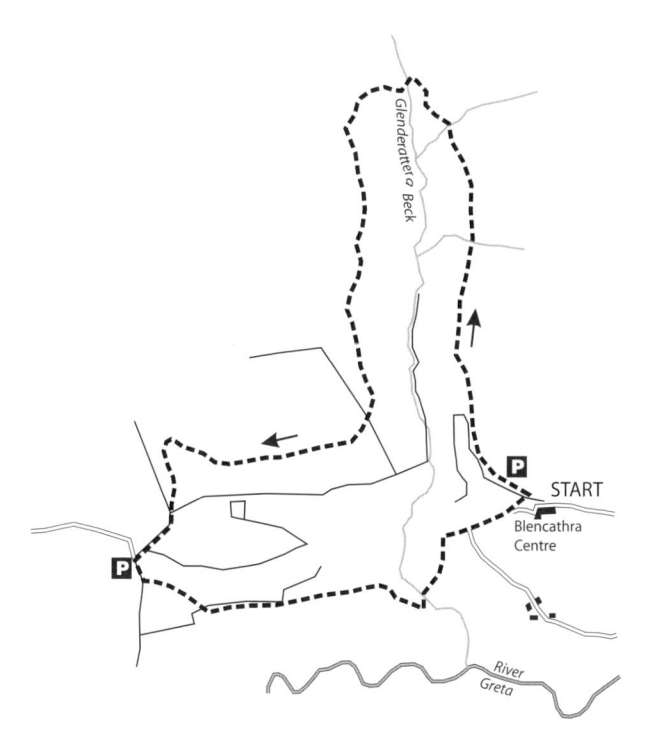

mine workings on the valley floor far below. As you start to draw level with these remains, you have to ford a small beck below a waterfall – a straightforward undertaking in all but the wettest of weather. The track drops slightly to cross Roughten Gill via a bridge. Soon after passing a sheepfold over to the left, you cross two wooden bridges in quick succession. The track now passes through a gate and begins to climb gently beside a drystone wall.

Over the years, lead, zinc and barytes have been mined in the Glenderaterra valley. The northern workings that you see in the valley bottom as you

SHORT WALKS

head up the track were part of what was first called the Glenderaterra Mine and later became the Brundholme Mine. Mining started here in the 19th century and, although the returns were never great, work continued until 1920.

About 250 metres beyond the gate, as you draw level with a gap in the wall on your right, turn left along a faint, grassy path heading in the general direction of Lonscale Fell. This quickly swings left, climbing all the time. Turn left at a junction with a clear track. This climbs briefly before contouring the fellside, high above Glenderaterra Beck. The ground on your left plummets steeply to the valley. Just after a rocky section, you emerge from the valley to be greeted by an impressive panorama. From the left, the view includes Clough Head, High Rigg and Bleaberry Fell. As you pass through the next gate, Derwentwater also comes into view as do the fells to the west of the lake. It's easy to switch off and assume there is nothing but uniform grass slopes between here and the Gale Road car park, which you can see ahead of you now. But the track conceals a pleasant surprise; hidden from view until the very last moment is a lovely, tree-lined ravine through which Whit Beck flows.

After going through a kissing-gate, follow the wall on your right until you reach the car park. Don't go through any of the gates here; instead, turn sharp left along a wide track with a fence/wall on your right. This track skirts the northern edge of Latrigg.

Having dropped to a rough lane, turn left. Almost immediately, bear right and walk downhill for about 150 metres. Turn left along a trail through the trees – signposted Derwent Folds and Blencathra. Cross the footbridge back over the Glenderaterra Beck. The stony, tree-lined path leads to a white-washed farmhouse.

Turn right along the lane here and, when it swings right, cross the stile up to your left. A faint path heads up to a kissing-gate in the field corner. Beyond this, continue uphill through the trees. Head diagonally across a small field to reach some buildings. Turn left, heading uphill on the track between them. Watch carefully for the next small signpost where you should turn left again. Go through the gate at the top of this path and turn left to return to the parking area. ◆

THE GERMAN MINERS

There are signs of mining throughout the Lake District, but it is the fells surrounding Keswick that bare some of the most obvious scars of the search for minerals. Copper, graphite, lead, coal, slate, cobalt, zinc and even silver have all been mined here, some possibly since Roman times, but it was in the 16th century that the industry really took off.

German miners, at that time the best in Europe, were invited to England by Elizabeth I in 1564. Employed by the Company of Mines Royal, they established copper and lead mines throughout Cumbria, the centre of operations being Keswick. At first, there was some discord between the immigrants and the locals, and the miners were, at one time, forced to flee to Derwent Isle on Derwent Water after several of them were murdered. But they brought prosperity – and a touch of the exotic – to the area, and were quickly accepted. By 1600, at least 60 miners had married local women, and their anglicised family names, including Stanger and Hindmarch, can still be found in the local phone book today.

Short Walks

3

Souther Fell

Start/Finish: Phone box in Mungrisdale (NY361303)
Distance: 7.6km (4¾ miles)
Height gain: 348m (1,140ft)
Type of walk: Valley track; open fell, boggy in places
Refreshments: Mill Inn, Mungrisdale

Souther Fell (522m) is probably one of the least visited of the Lakeland fells, but its pleasant, grassy top gives great views of Blencathra, the Pennines, the eastern fells and even across to some of the central fells. The route up is along the River Glenderamackin followed by a short, easy climb along the fell's grassy south-eastern ridge. The most difficult part of the walk is probably the descent, which is steep in places. Watch out for the ghostly riders that haunt the fell at midsummer!

AS YOU FOLLOW THE LANE THAT HEADS WEST from the old red phone box in Mungrisdale, you will pass the pretty cottage of Bannerdale View on your left. Go through the large gate and on to a wide track. About 40 metres after crossing a narrow wooden bridge, leave the track by turning left along a narrow path beside the River Glenderamackin. The turning is easy to miss, so make sure you keep your eyes peeled for it. You now follow the river for the next 2.8km (1¾ miles). The path is clear, but it does get soggy after wet weather.

Just after the path swings SE at a bend in the river, watch out for a plank bridge crossing the channel below you. To reach it, you will need to take a narrow path to your

IN THE LAKE DISTRICT

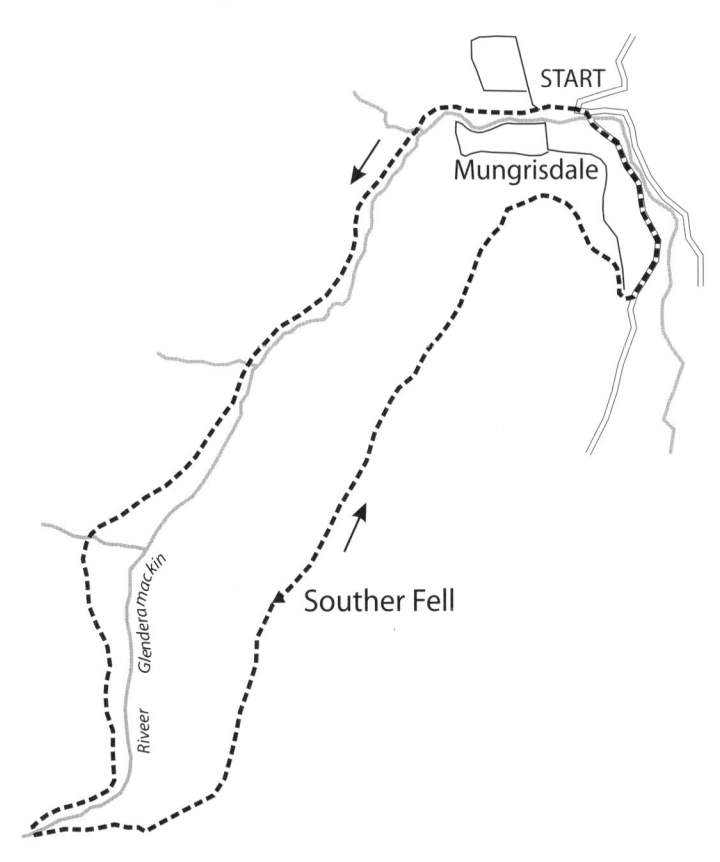

left. Watch carefully for it because it is easy to miss from the main path. Cross the Glenderamackin via the bridge and ascend the path on the other side in an easterly direction. As you climb, take some time to look back at the impressive view of Foule Crag and Sharp Edge on Blencathra. At the top of the climb, you reach a crossing of paths in a grassy pass. Turn left here along a wide,

21

Short Walks

> grassy track ascending Souther Fell. You soon reach the flat top and, coming to a boggy area, bear left at a faint fork to visit a cairn on the western edge of Souther Fell.

It was on **Souther Fell**, on Midsummer Eve in 1735, that the servant of William Lancaster, of Blake Hills Farm, saw a troop of ghostly horsemen crossing the fell. Exactly two years later, Mr Lancaster and his family saw the same sight. All of them were ridiculed when they told of the huge numbers involved, ascending a stretch of the fell that no rider would attempt.

So, a few years later, again on Midsummer Eve, Mr Lancaster took 26 companions with him to witness the spectacle. They all saw the horsemen and even went to investigate the ground they had ridden on, finding no sign of hoofprints or other evidence that horses had passed that way.

The story has been well documented through the years – by William Hutchinson in his 1793 work *The History of the County of Cumberland* and by Harriet Martineau's *Guide to the English Lakes* in 1855. Even William Wordsworth recalls the legend in *An Evening Walk*, talking of "strange apparitions" that "mocked the shepherd's sight... Of horsemen-shadows moving to and fro".

> To get to the true summit, bear right at the cairn (ENE) along a faint path. In a few minutes you regain the main path along the ridge. Another few minutes and you reach the easy-to-miss summit – marked only by a few rocks. From the top, follow the faint, grassy path downhill (NE). It gets pretty steep in places. Just when you think you are almost back in Mungrisdale, your direct descent suddenly stops as you reach a post with a white marker arrow on it. Turn right here along a narrow, level route through the bracken. This eventually descends to a road.
>
> Turn left at the road to go through the gate. Pass the Mill Inn and then turn left at the T-junction. The telephone box where the walk started is just ahead on the left. ◆

IN THE LAKE DISTRICT

4

GRAYSTONES AND BROOM FELL

Start/Finish: Scawgill Bridge, about 3km NW of the Whinlatter Visitor Centre on the B5292. There is room for a few cars beside the road on the north side of the bridge (NY177257)
Distance: 6km (3¾ miles)
Height gain: 433m (1,420ft)
Type of walk: Open fell, pathless at times; forest track
Refreshments: Siskins Café at Whinlatter Visitor Centre

*If you're looking for a short, relatively easy fell walk and you want to escape the crowds, the lonely, grassy tops of **Graystones** (456m) and **Broom Fell** (510m) above the Whinlatter forests make an ideal choice. The route on to Graystones is steep, but, because you start at 232m above sea level, it isn't too long. Be warned though – the lower slopes on this walk are covered in thick bracken in summer, so you may want to keep your legs covered to avoid being attacked by ticks.*

GO THROUGH THE KISSING-GATE and, ignoring the signposted footpath straight ahead, turn left. Almost immediately, bear right – along the faint, narrow path that comes off the overgrown old quarry track. In just a few strides, this climbs some loose slate and then swings right immediately. The path is quite overgrown, so watch carefully for it; don't be tempted by any steeper paths heading up to the left. It climbs very gently at first, even dropping briefly at one point as it makes its way towards the edge of the forest. When you reach the trees, follow the path as it swings left to climb alongside a wall on your

Short Walks

right. The ascent, through bracken at first, now becomes a lot steeper.

Nearing the top, you reach a rocky outcrop. Ignore the path crossing yours here; continue straight up the fellside, passing to the left of the rocks before the path swings right again to regain the line of the old wall. Ignore any subsequent paths crossing yours. Continue uphill until the gradient eases considerably and the views to the north begin to open out. Leave the path now by crossing the wall on the right. Graystones is a rather knobbly top, so it isn't obvious at first where the highest point is. It's marked by a cairn though, so if you make for the high ground, you should be able to spot it. Note that it's on the eastern side of the wall. (There is also a cairn to the west of the wall.)

IN THE LAKE DISTRICT

From the summit, you can see across the **Solway Firth** into Scotland on a clear day. Over to the east, Skiddaw is visible, and you can also see the tall cairn on the summit of Broom Fell, your next target. To the SE, the pyramid-like peak of Grisedale Pike stands out. This 701m top forms part of the Coledale Horseshoe, one of the classic Lakeland mountain rounds which also includes Eel Crag and Hopegill Head.

Pick up a narrow trail through the grass (NNE). This becomes very faint, but if you maintain a roughly NNE line, you should reach a fence coming down from the left. Continue downhill with this on your left until you reach a dip. Carefully cross the short section of low wooden fence here and then turn right along a faint path. The ground is damp in places as you follow the edge of the forest over undulating ground. The trees come to an abrupt end when you reach a junction of fences and walls at a dip in the ridge. Leave the security of the fence/wall here and head steeply up the slope straight in front of you on a faint path (ENE). Crossing boggy ground along the way, this winds its way to the cairn on the summit of Broom Fell, from where you get an uninterrupted view of the Skiddaw massif, including Longside Edge, the ridge running to the west of the summit screes. There is a small shelter to the right of the cairn should you need it.

Do not cross the stile in the fence; instead, turn right at the cairn (SSW) along a faint, grassy path heading downhill beside the tumbledown wall. As you descend, the pleasant, grassy slope gives way to bracken. The path is hard to make out in the dense vegetation, but it is still there, keeping close to the old wall.

When you reach a wire-topped fence running across the wall, carefully cross it. A pile of rocks on either side makes life a bit easier. Continue following the wall downhill, on top of the old stones at first, but then on a damp path between the wall and the young conifers on

Short Walks

your right. Cross a small beck and then follow the path steeply uphill. It keeps close to the wall for just a few more metres and then swings right, through the bracken. Watch your footing here because the path is narrow and the steep drop on your right is hidden by the vegetation. Having fought your way through the bracken for a few more hundred metres, you cross another beck – this one slightly wider than the previous one. Before long, you walk parallel with a wall on your left and eventually come out on to a wide forest track.

Turn right and then, when you reach the road, turn right again to return to the parking area. ◆

Drystone walls

Drystone walls are an integral part of the Cumbrian landscape – creating the small enclosures that are so typical of Lakeland valleys, and running for seemingly endless miles on the open fell-tops. Built without mortar or cement, some of them date back to the late 13th century when the Cistercian monks of Furness Abbey farmed the region, but most were built during the Enclosure movement of the 18th and 19th centuries.

The walls are built on a foundation of two parallel rows of large boulders on either side of a trench. The sides are then built up and the inside is filled with smaller stones. At regular intervals, a layer of 'throughstones' is placed across the entire width of the wall to strengthen it. Walls tend to be wider at the bottom than at the top – for stability. They are generally topped with a row of slanting or vertical stones, known as 'cam-stones', to discourage sheep from climbing over the wall.

IN THE LAKE DISTRICT

5

HIGH PIKE

Start/Finish: Car park in Hesket Newmarket,
next to Denton House B&B (NY342386)
Distance: 10.6km (6½ miles)
Height gain: 497m (1,630ft)
Type of walk: Farm paths; grassy paths and track on the fells; good tracks
Refreshments: Oddfellows Arms pub, Old Smithy café and Watermill restaurant, all in Caldbeck

The rounded grassy hills of the northern fells often seem a long way removed from the better known, craggier fells further south. Even on a decent length outing such as this one, you'll not have much in the way of rock under your boots and there's a good chance that you will sometimes walk for hours without seeing another soul. There's a sense of solitude and 'openness' that is more akin to the North Pennines than the Lake District.

*This route on to **High Pike**, starting from the pretty village of Hesket Newmarket, is typical of the Northern Fells in all senses. It heads up on to the open fells via fields, rough grazing land and some old mine workings. The climbing is reasonably easy and well spaced-out, but the paths, which may be wet in places, are not always clear. The return is via Potts Gill and Nether Row – mostly on good tracks and paths after the initial descent from the summit.*

You should be able to see a bench on the open area at the back of the car park in Hesket Newmarket. Behind this is the path on which the walk starts – signposted Wood

Short Walks

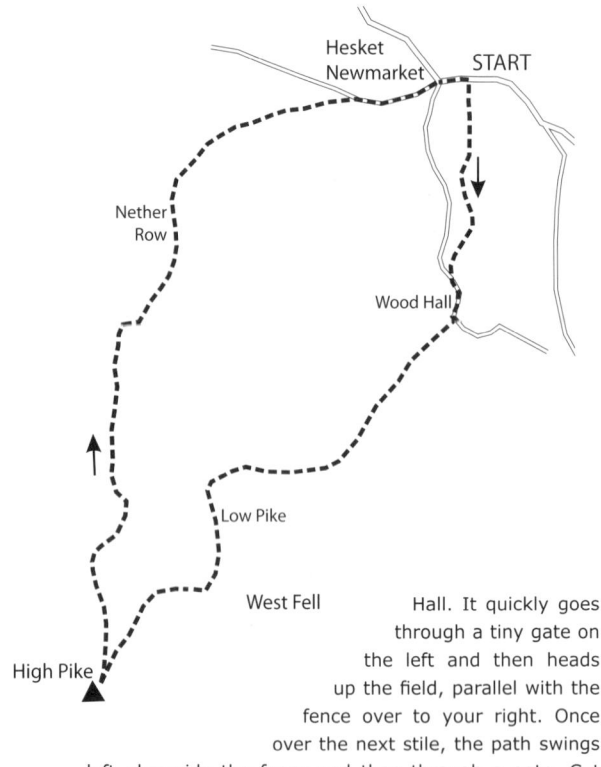

Hall. It quickly goes through a tiny gate on the left and then heads up the field, parallel with the fence over to your right. Once over the next stile, the path swings left alongside the fence and then through a gate. Cut diagonally across the next field and through the gate in the far corner. Head for the fence corner directly ahead and then cross the stile on the left. The faint path goes diagonally across the next field, over another stile and then continues in the same direction to reach a stile next to a metal gate about 50 metres to the right of an old shed. Cross straight over the grassy track – which leads to Stott Ghyll – and climb the stile opposite. Go through a small gate on the other side of this field and then walk alongside the fence on the right to access the road via a large metal gate in a wall.

Turn left along the asphalt. Having passed between the farm buildings at Wood Hall, the road performs a sharp left-hand bend. Immediately after it does so, go through the gate on your right. A faint track passes to the right of a small pond. As you make your way up to the fence, you will see two stiles on either side of two large metal gates. Cross the one on the left. Head SW across this pathless rough pasture, crossing a shallow gully as you climb gently. You will find a ladder stile next to a gate in a wall, about 200 metres to the right of a narrow belt of conifers. Once over this, you are on access land.

Cross the tiny beck immediately in front of you and then pick up a grassy track heading away from the wall, making for the old mine workings at the base of the fell (SSW, veering SW). Ignore any narrow paths off and when the track forks, keep right. Having passed to the left of the remains of a drystone construction, ignore one path off to the left and then keep straight ahead (WNW, veering WSW) when another faint track goes off to the right. Cross a damp area and then climb the steep, grassy slope to reach a clear track, along which you turn right. This now climbs gently for about 150 metres.

Just as the track dips slightly, bear left along a grassy track climbing away from it at a 45-degree angle. This eventually curves round to skirt the edge of some fenced mine workings and then assumes a SW course. As you later draw level with a rough track heading down to the left near some more old workings, turn right along a narrow, but clear path heading more steeply uphill (W). Turn left when you reach a clear ridge track (SSW). With good views across the Solway Firth to the right, you climb to a large shelter, which used to be a shepherd's hut. Now

Short Walks

swing half-left (S) to reach the summit furniture, which includes a bench and trig pillar.

Having rested at the top, retrace your steps to the old shepherd's hut and then, instead of taking the path to the right on which you approached the summit, keep straight ahead on a wide path heading down the fell in the general direction of the village of Caldbeck far below (N). Turn right along the track at the bottom of this slope.

Soon after passing some old mine workings at the top of Potts Gill, turn left at a crossing of tracks (NNW). Go straight across one clear, stony track and then join another coming down from the left. Having passed a few steep-sided piles of rubble, you will see a small, square mound to the right of the track (it has a stone base and a grassy top). Just before this, take the grassy track on the left (NNW, later swinging NE). On reaching a wall corner, keep heading in roughly the same direction, towards the buildings at Nether Row, and you will pick up a track running alongside the wall. This goes through a couple of gates and eventually swings left, becoming a surfaced lane.

Mining in **Potts Gill** started in the 1870s, when prospectors unsuccessfully searched for lead and copper, but found only barytes. Large-scale mining really only took off in the 20th century when the market for this mineral improved. The area was particularly busy during World War Two when barytes were needed for munitions. An aerial ropeway was used to transport the baryte from the mine to the road at Nether Row, just over 1km (½ mile) away. Operations ceased in 1966.

Once you have passed all the buildings in Nether Row, turn right along a track when the road bends left. Cross straight over the next track and the subsequent stile to access a grassy path between a wall and a fence. After the next stile, continue in the same direction, towards the red buildings at Street Head. Cross a stile to the right of a gate and continue between the wall and the fence. After the next stile, swing left and go through a gate to the immediate left of the red building.

Turn right at the road and then right again at the T-junction in Hesket Newmarket. The car park is about 200 metres on your right, soon after the Old Crown pub.

The **Old Crown** in Hesket Newmarket is well-known for being Britain's first co-operatively owned pub and serves a selection of popular ales brewed in the village's co-operatively owned brewery. Jim and Liz Fearnley opened Hesket Newmarket Brewery in 1988. When Jim retired in 1999, villagers feared the business would be swallowed up by a larger brewery or even closed down, so 58 of them got together and formed a co-operative. They bought the brewery, which is still a successful business, producing popular beers such as Great Cockup Porter and Doris' 90th Birthday Ale. When, a few years later, the Old Crown was placed on the market, locals again feared it could be taken over by a large brewery or pub chain, so 125 regulars clubbed together and bought it. ◆

Short Walks

6

Gowbarrow and Aira Force

Start/Finish: National Trust pay and display car park
at Aira Force (NY400200)
Distance: 6.4km (4 miles)
Height gain: 353m (1,157ft)
Type of walk: Rough beckside route; hill paths
Refreshments: Small café next to the car park

It often seems that some of the best views in the Lakes are from the minor tops. **Gowbarrow**, *at only 481m, is a good example. Heading up past dramatic* **Aira Force** *at first, the route then does a circuit of the top of the fell. It's a lovely excursion that visits the summit and then comes round the eastern side of the fell, but it's when you reach the southern edge that you will be stopped in your tracks... The view down Ullswater towards the Helvellyn range is simply magnificent. The word breathtaking is often used a little too liberally, but it's hard to resist that sharp intake of breath as the lake is properly revealed.*

GO THROUGH THE GAP in the National Trust stone construction at the far end of the car park and then, having passed through a couple of gates and crossed a tiny beck, you reach an area of ancient yews and towering conifers. Turn left here, away from the iron railings on the right, to slowly ascend, with the beck on your right, to a bench. Turn right to descend the steep stone staircase to the base of the powerful falls, feeling the spray from the water even on calm days.

William Wordsworth was a frequent visitor to this area, and wrote three

IN THE LAKE DISTRICT

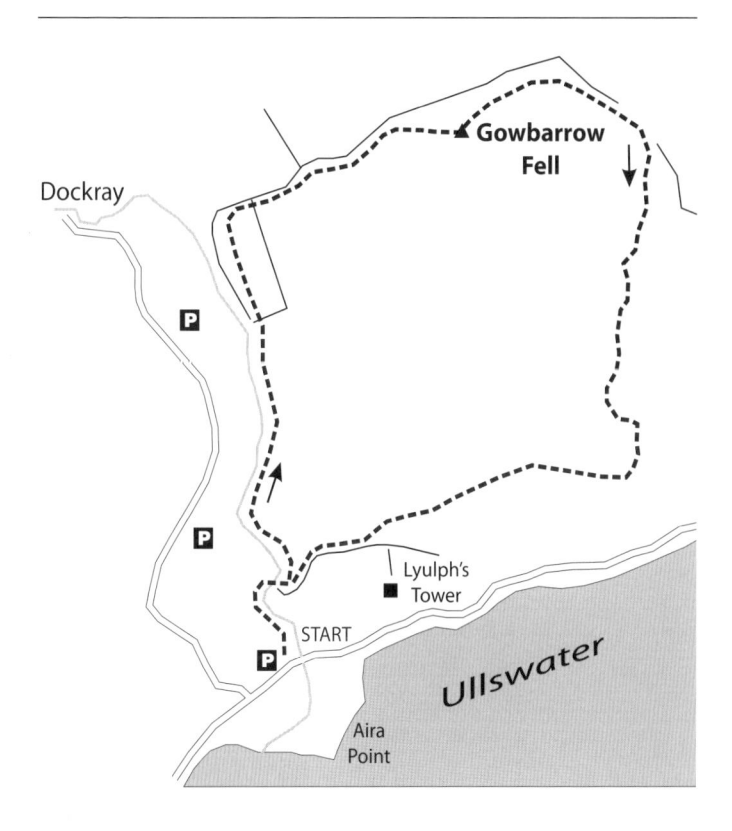

poems about Aira Force, the most well known being *The Somnambulist*. This tells the local legend of two lovers who were parted by war. As the knight went off to fight, his sweetheart was left at home, worrying about him. Her anxiety led her to start sleepwalking along the edge of the steep Aira ravine. When the knight returned, he discovered her asleep and in this precarious position. He touched her and she awoke, losing her balance and falling into the ravine. Needless to say, as in all good legends, the damsel died and the knight built himself a cell on the river bank to mourn his loss.

The woodland at the southern base of Gowbarrow is also said to have inspired Wordsworth to write his most famous poem, *Daffodils*. Having walked through the woods with him on April 15, 1802, his sister Dorothy noted in her diary: "I never saw daffodils so beautiful they grew among the mossy stones about and about them, some rested their heads upon these stones as on a pillow for weariness and the rest tossed and reeled and danced and seemed as if they verily laughed with the wind that blew upon them over the lake, they looked so gay ever dancing ever changing." Two years later, he used Dorothy's observations as the basis of a poem, the first line of which is probably one of the most famous lines in English poetry… "I wandered lonely as a cloud…"

Cross the bridge at the bottom and then turn left immediately – up another steep, stone stairway, joining a path coming in from the right. Back on the main path, there is quite a bit of clambering to be done as you wend your way upstream. In a couple of hundred metres, you will see a path branching off to the left to a wooden footbridge below. Ignore this, and continue with the beck on your left. The woods start to thin out after you pass through gap in a wall and then disappear entirely after a gate in a fence.

Just before you reach another gate – a small, wooden gate beside a larger farm gate – turn right to start climbing on a faint path. Cross the ladder stile and head steeply uphill with the wall on your left. After about half-an-hour of uphill slog, the path finally levels off slightly and swings right towards the trig point.

Descend NE from the summit and follow the path round to the remains of an old shooting hut on the eastern edge of the fell. Bear right here. About 20 minutes beyond the ruin, you round the side of a crag and are suddenly faced with one of the most magnificent panoramas in the eastern Lakes. The western expanse of Ullswater is revealed with the dark, craggy Helvellyn range in the

IN THE LAKE DISTRICT

> background. The level path continues for a short while and then drops gently to a fence.

As you descend, you will see what looks like a medieval tower below. This is **Lyulph's Tower** and isn't as old as it looks; it was actually built as a shooting lodge in 1780.

> Once through the gate, bear left at the next junction to descend through woodland to cross a bridge over Aira Beck. Climb the steps on the other side and bear left through a gap in some iron railings. It's now a five-minute woodland stroll back to the car park.

Many of the trees in the arboretum around Aira Force were planted by the Howard family of Greystoke. They were lords of the manor from the late Middle Ages until they sold the land to the National Trust in 1906. The fine specimens include a Douglas fir that is said to be the tallest tree in Cumbria, some ancient yews and a Chilean pine or 'Monkey Puzzle' tree. There are also two huge sitka spruces on the eastern side of the beck. A much maligned species due to over-planting in British plantations during the 20th century, this pair dates back to 1846. The largest has a girth of more than six metres, placing it in the top seven largest sitka spruces in the UK. ◆

SHORT WALKS

7

RED TARN

Start/Finish: Main car park in Glenridding (NY386169)
Distance: 10.3km (6½ miles)
Height gain: 631m (2,070ft)
Type of walk: Mostly good fell and valley paths throughout, steep in places
Refreshments: Choice of cafés, pubs and restaurants in Glenridding

*Save this walk for a lovely, sunny day, and your efforts will be more than fairly rewarded in terms of great views and atmospheric locations. It ascends Birkhouse Moor (702m) via Mires Beck, using a fairly steep, but well pitched path. It continues easily to moody **Red Tarn** at the foot of Helvellyn's forbidding eastern cliffs before dropping down to Glenridding Beck. A delightful leat route, hugging the side of the fell high above the valley floor, then takes you most of the way back to Glenridding.*

FROM THE MAIN CAR PARK, head back out on to the main road and turn right. Turn right again along a surfaced lane immediately after crossing the bridge over Glenridding Beck – towards Mires Beck and Helvellyn. About 100 metres after passing the last building on the right, bear right at a fork in the track – towards Gillside, Miresbeck, Greenside and Helvellyn.

When you reach a minor road, turn left and then, almost immediately, pick up the gravel path to the right of the road. This soon joins up with a wider track as it heads uphill. On reaching a junction of tracks at a gate, keep straight on up (left-hand option) following the Mires Beck

IN THE LAKE DISTRICT

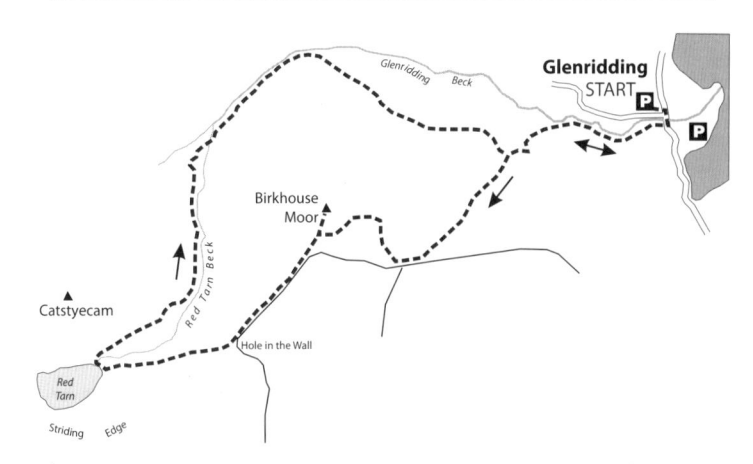

path. In another 100 metres, you will see a white gate ahead on the track; just before you reach it, follow the main track as it bends sharp right. This soon climbs to a gate and ladder stile, beyond which you turn sharp left to cross a plank bridge. You now begin climbing beside Mires Beck, crossing to the eastern bank early on via a ford.

Although it's a straightforward path, it can be a bit of a tedious slog at first, but then you reach the ridge and are met by a glorious sight – the dark gullies and airy ridges along the north-western face of St Sunday Crag. To the right of this are the cliffs of Fairfield. Look to your left and you can see the High Street range. This is the reason why we trudge our weary way up the boring bits!

The path now swings right to follow the wall uphill for a while. The route on the ground then deviates from what you see on the map because, instead of following the wall straight up, it begins a zigzagging ascent. Keep to the constructed path at all times; don't be tempted to cut any corners.

SHORT WALKS

You only leave the path briefly to take a short detour to the cairn on Birkhouse Moor. You do this just after you get your first, uninterrupted sighting of Catstye Cam and Helvellyn's eastern cliffs – and just before the path swings left. At this point, to reach the cairn, turn right along the faint path through the grass. Once you've visited the cairn marking the summit, return to the main path and continue uphill. The ascent is soon over and you find yourself striding out along a ridge with the wall on your left. As you near a ladder stile, turn right, away from the wall, along a clear track heading straight towards Helvellyn's cliffs. When the constructed track negotiates its way through a rocky area, bear left along a narrower path to reach Red Tarn.

Sitting at the foot of the dark cliffs, this is a great place to rest and watch the walkers lining the two arêtes that cradle **Red Tarn** – Striding Edge to the south and Swirral Edge to the north. Striding Edge, in particular, has a ferocious reputation. There have been many accidents, many of them fatal, along this narrow ridge over the years. It becomes particularly treacherous in icy or windy conditions.

The exit from Striding Edge is marked by a plaque telling the story of artist Charles Gough, whose body was found in 1805 at the base of the crags beneath this spot. His rotting remains had been guarded for three months by his dog, a story that inspired Sir Walter Scott to write the poem Climbed the Dark Brow of Mighty Helvellyn and William Wordsworth to pen Fidelity.

When you cross the outlet stream, bear right, away from the tarn, and rejoin the main path, which swings left. A few metres later, at a fork, turn right. You now begin descending, gradually at first, along a clear, wide track. About one mile from the tarn, you cross Red Tarn Beck via a small, wooden bridge and then continue with Glenridding Beck on your left.

IN THE LAKE DISTRICT

You will soon see part of the old **Greenside Mine** workings. Lead was discovered here in the middle of the 17th century, with Dutch adventurers driving the first level in the 1690s and then transporting the dressed ore to the Stoneycroft smelter near Keswick, 16km (10 miles) away. Serious development didn't begin until 1822 when the Greenside Mining Company was formed. By 1849, there were 300 workers here, making it the largest lead mine in England.

The mine operated until 1962, when it became uneconomic. In its lifetime, it had produced about 2.4 million tons of lead ore and 2 million ounces of silver. After its closure, it was at one time leased to the Atomic Energy Authority who carried out non-nuclear explosions here to test seismic equipment. Some of the converted mine buildings are now used as outdoor education centres.

> About 200 metres after passing and ignoring a bridge over the beck, you will see a faint, grassy path off to the left. Ignore this. Instead, stay on the clear, level path that follows the line of a disused leat for just under 1km (½ mile).

This leat would once have been used to carry water for the mining operations at Greenside. The mine was the first in Britain to use electrical winding and underground haulage, generating its own electricity by means of water turbines.

The water was supplied by the damming of nearby tarns. One of them, in Keppel Cove, burst its banks in October 1927, bringing devastation to Glenridding below. None of the villagers was killed, but many buildings were destroyed. In fact, the promontory on which the modern steamer pier is situated is formed from the flood debris.

The leat hugs the hillside at about the 330m contour and, as you stride out early on, you can look down into the cool, blue pools of Glenridding Beck, which flows through a rocky gorge at this point in its journey down to Ullswater. Further along, the track provides ever improving views of Glenridding and, on the other side of the lake, Place Fell.

Do not leave the line of the leat until you come to a wall apparently blocking your way ahead. Bear left here to descend a rocky path. At the bottom of the short descent, turn right. Cross a ladder stile beside a gate and then retrace your steps to Glenridding, remembering to turn left at the next junction and then, almost immediately, turn right along a wide track just before the bridge across the beck. ◆

FELL PONIES

Cumbria's fell ponies, most commonly seen on the northern and eastern fells, have been wandering these hills for many hundreds of years, if not millennia. Their history can be traced back to the Romans, when indigenous ponies bred with the horses introduced by the occupiers and their foreign mercenaries. The result of this and subsequent cross-breeding with the Galloway breed and the Welsh cob is a sturdy, but lively little animal that has served many purposes over the years.

At one time, shepherds would have used fell ponies for rounding up their flocks. Before that, the Vikings used them for ploughing. It was only in the 13th century, with the rise of the wool trade, that they began to be used as pack animals on a large scale, carrying merchandise along old routes that still exist today. Come the Industrial Revolution and they began carrying lead and iron ore from the fells to the smelting works on the north-east coast. They would have travelled in 'trains' of up to 20, covering up to 240 miles a week.

Although they may look wild, all of these ponies belong to someone, but they run free on hundreds of acres of common land. They are brought down from the fells only twice a year – in the late spring, when the mares are gathered for foaling; and in the autumn, when the colt foals are sold at auction.

IN THE LAKE DISTRICT

8

WANSFELL RIDGE FROM KIRKSTONE PASS

Start/Finish: Large car park opposite Kirkstone Pass Inn
(NY401080)
Distance: 10.5km (6½ miles)
Height gain: 616m (2,020ft)
Type of walk: Good track; open fell, pathless at times
Refreshments: Kirkstone Pass Inn

Wansfell Pike is a popular top that is normally climbed from Ambleside, but what many walkers don't realise is that this isn't the highest point on Wansfell; to the north is a pleasant, quiet ridge path that leads up to the true summit (489m) about 1.5km (1 mile) away. To avoid the honeypot that is Ambleside, our route starts from Kirkstone Pass, following a track downhill from near the top of The Struggle. The only time you are likely to encounter other walkers is on the climb on to Wansfell Pike itself. From here, you follow the ridge to the summit and then drop down to the A592. The final part of the day is probably the most difficult – a slow slog up Broad End without the aid of paths before dropping steeply back down to Kirkstone Pass. At 569m, the top of this final climb marks the highest point on the walk.

ON LEAVING THE CAR PARK, turn right along the main road and then right again along the road to Ambleside. Soon after the road crosses a small beck, go through a large wooden gate on your left. The rough, muddy track curves around the head of the valley and then begins descending, almost imperceptibly, with Stock Ghyll on

SHORT WALKS

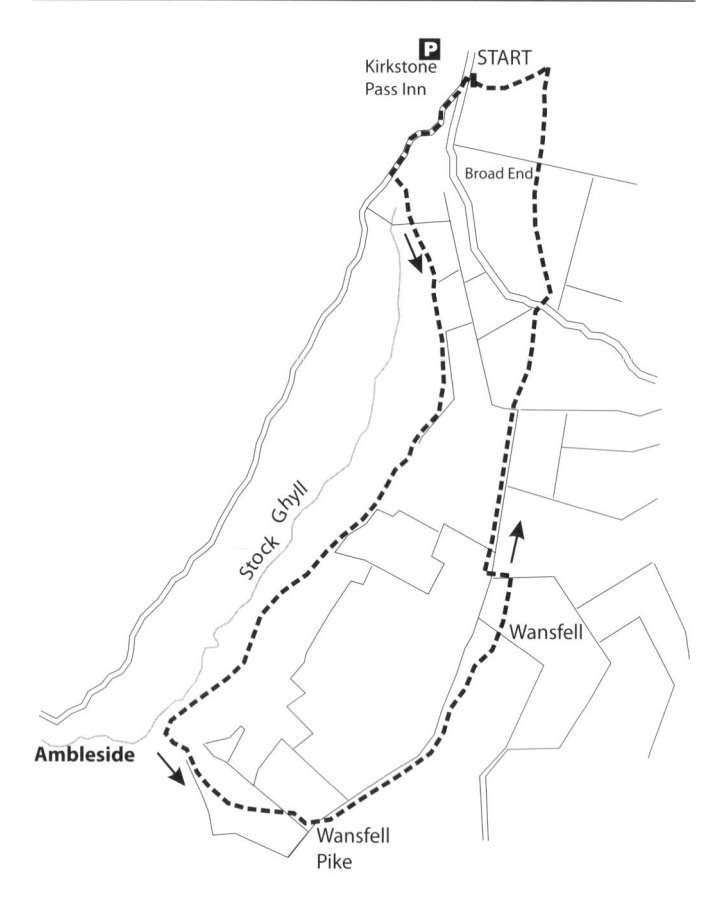

the right. You can see the working slate quarry on Red Screes up to your right and, in the distance, the first of the high fells to appear belong to the Coniston group. Eventually, the track becomes a pleasant grassy lane and is channelled between two drystone walls. On reaching Grove Farm, it goes over to asphalt, as you continue following it downhill. The views to the right open up now to include Crinkle Crags, Bow Fell and the Langdales.

About 500 metres after passing a cottage called Mountain View, cross the stile in the wall on your left to begin climbing the well used path on to Wansfell Pike. This soon passes through a kissing-gate, after which you swing left to continue the climb on an obvious path. You end up clambering on bare rock for the last few metres of the ascent, but otherwise it's a straightforward ascent.

From the summit, there's a mesmerising view down Windermere, dotted with boats, and then down the south Cumbrian estuaries that lead into Morecambe Bay. The attractive, rounded hills in the distance – to the SE – are the Howgills.

Cross the ladder stile in the fence and turn left along the ridge route. The narrow trail follows every twist and turn and bump and dip of the wall to the left. About 500 metres beyond Wansfell Pike, it crosses another wall running perpendicular to the ridge wall. Then, in another 300 metres, it begins to swing away from the ridge wall to climb a few small hummocks on the way to the true summit of Wansfell.

The top, rather dull in comparison with Wansfell Pike, is marked by a prominent cairn, beyond which you continue in roughly the same direction (NNE) to reach a wall. Turn left here and walk with the wall on your right until you reach the ridge wall. Now turn right, over the wooden pallet fence and follow the faint trail alongside the wall on your left. Eventually, the wall on your left ends, but the narrow path continues beyond the stile in the perpendicular wall. Crossing boggy ground, it becomes very faint at times, but you should maintain a northerly direction, climbing slightly.

Turn right at the road and then, almost immediately, cross

over to go through the wooden gate on your left. You now need to make your way up Broad End. If you look straight up the steep, grassy fell ahead, you will see a gap in the line of rocky outcrops at the top of the slope (NNW). This is your next target, but there are no obvious paths to guide you. Beyond the gap, keep heading NNW to gain the high ground of the broad ridge. It's slow going, but about 800 metres beyond the road, you will reach a wall with a stile in it. Cross this and continue uphill (N).

About 500 metres beyond the stile, watch for another wall over to your left. The path back down to Kirkstone Pass is on the other side of this wall, so you need to make your way over to it and cross at one of many gaps. Then turn left to head steeply down the rough, rocky path. The gradient eases and you cross a couple of stiles before the path drops you back at the road, opposite the Kirkstone Pass car park.

In 2004, *The Westmorland Gazette* reported that a teenager living at the **Kirkstone Pass Inn**, had captured the "otherworldly outlines" of a young girl on his mobile phone while he was locked in a disused room there. The remote, centuries-old travellers' inn already had several ghost stories associated with it. There are tales of the spirit of a woman who died while trying to cross the pass in a snowstorm, and of a lost hiker who worked at the hotel and now plays poltergeist tricks there. A coachman dressed in 17th-century clothing mysteriously appeared in a photograph taken in front of the inn in 1993. And a woman hanged for murdering her child is said to haunt the pass. Ghosthunters believe the apparition seen on the boy's mobile phone may have been the ghost of the murdered child. "We were messing around and my mum and some other people shut me in there," the teenager explained to the newspaper. "I heard heavy breathing near my ears. I was scared – it's really horrible up there – so I used the light on my phone to try and get out. When I got back downstairs I realised I'd been videoing. I watched it and I saw a girl with a light behind her but there's no light up there at night, it's totally dark." ◆

IN THE LAKE DISTRICT

9

PLACE FELL FROM HOWTOWN

Start: Howtown pier (NY443199)
Finish: Glenridding pier (NY401080)
Public transport: Linear route using the Ullswater 'Steamer'
Distance: 11.3km (7 miles)
Height gain: 633m (2,075ft)
Type of walk: Popular lakeside path; fell paths, boggy and indistinct in places; roadside walking
Refreshments: Howtown Hotel; choice of cafés, pubs and restaurants in Glenridding

The top of **Place Fell** *(657m) is another busy spot – it seems to be on the itinerary of just about every hill-walker passing through Glenridding and Patterdale, drawn, no doubt, by the wonderful views of the mightier ranges to the west. But that's not to say the entire fell is crowded; if you know where to look, there are still several paths that see relatively few visitors.*

This linear route, which makes use of the Ullswater 'Steamer', ascends via Sleet Fell, a little-known hill to the NE of Place Fell itself. It then approaches the trig point from the N, avoiding the well-walked path across Hart Crag. The descent uses the steep, well-trodden Boredale Hause path to leave the fell, but then finds an alternative, quieter route that leads almost all the way down to Side Farm near Patterdale.

The walk is mostly on grass, including the steep ascent of Sleet Fell, but

Short Walks

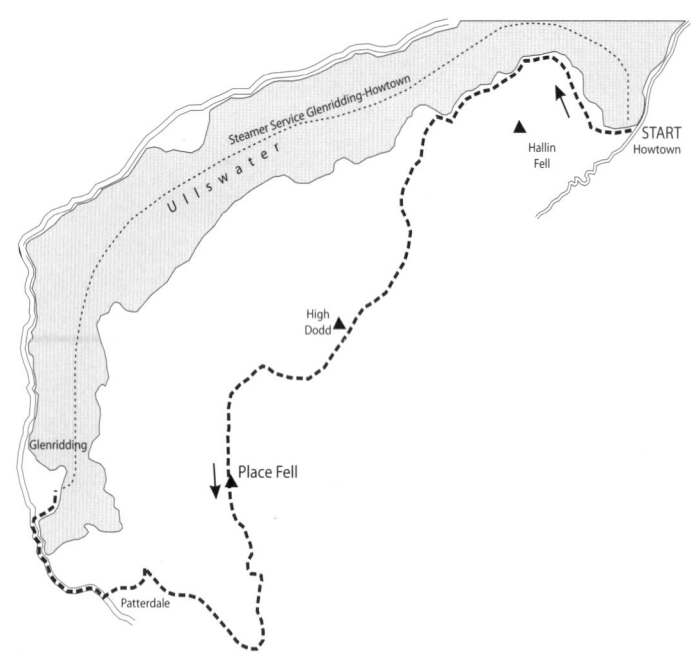

there are some rockier and stonier sections. The paths are mostly clear on the ground, although the route from the sheepfold to the trig point is boggy and indistinct in places.

HAVING CAUGHT THE STEAMER FROM GLENRIDDING, get off in Howtown and turn right at the end of the pier to cross the wooden footbridge – towards Sandwick. When you reach an asphalt lane, turn right and then turn left through another gate – towards Patterdale and Sandwick. At the top of the rise, go through the gate and turn right along a path at the base of Hallin Fell. You soon find yourself strolling along a lovely path above the lake. Gradually losing height, go through a kissing-gate

IN THE LAKE DISTRICT

to enter some woodland. When you leave the woods, the path veers away from the lake, climbing a gentle slope via a series of small gates. It then drops towards Sandwick. When you reach the beck, turn left and then cross the bridge. Turn left at the surfaced lane and, immediately after the last building on your right, turn right along a stony path.

After 320 metres, as you draw level with a kink in the wall on your right, turn left along a grassy path heading straight up the fell. This quickly splits and, when it does so, ignore the ditch-like path to the left. Take either of the other two options, although the left-hand route goes up to a bench, known as Peggy's Seat, that you may want to put to good use before launching your assault on the steep, grassy slope ahead. At the next clear fork, bear left to head uphill. The path is badly eroded in its early stages, but a zig-zagging route makes the ascent easier than it would otherwise be. Before you know it, the gradient eases and the path swings right to continue climbing more easily.

After making your way between some rocky outcrops, you reach a cairn on the edge of the ridge with good views down into Boredale directly below and across to Beda Fell, Steel Knotts and Loadpot Hill. Looking beyond Hallin Fell, the Pennines are clearly visible in the distance. Continue along this wonderful, grassy path, bypassing the next cairn up to your right. As the route skirts the eastern base of High Dodd, you will be joined by another path coming up from the valley. Having crossed some boggy ground, you eventually reach a bleakly located old sheepfold.

From here, most walkers continue straight up the fell on a wide path you can see heading SW, but our route uses a more circuitous, but less well trodden and more

Short Walks

interesting route... Head SW along the main path at first, but then, after 100 metres, bear right along a shallow groove. It doesn't look like a path at first, but it is, in fact, a right of way that has existed for many years. You have a magnificent view across to Blencathra as you make your way steadily uphill. At the top of the rise, you are greeted by a stunning panorama straight ahead – Catstycam and the dark, forbidding eastern cliffs and gullies of the Helvellyn range. The path becomes indistinct as it crosses some boggy patches, but just keep heading in the same direction (SW) until you cross two small becks in quick succession.

The path now swings left (S) to begin climbing again. Things remain damp underfoot at first, but then the path swings right on to higher ground. Just after Helvellyn makes a dramatic reappearance, you drop to a slightly clearer path. Turn left here (SSE). The path becomes rockier as you make your way uphill on the last significant ascent of the day. The trig point marking the top of Place Fell is to the left of the path, perched on top of a spiky lump of rock.

Beyond the summit, continue on the well-trodden path along the western edge of the fell. To avoid a loose, unpleasant scramble down a badly eroded section of path, turn right along a faint trail 360 metres beyond the trig point. Striding out with wonderful views down towards Brothers Water, you may be lucky enough to spot red deer grazing on these steep slopes. You soon meet up with the main path, along which you turn right. Much of the descent now is on a pitched path.

The fells to the east of Ullswater are home to England's oldest native herd of **red deer**, said to be the only herd that hasn't cross-bred with sika deer. The ancient deer forest itself is centred on The Nab, but the deer range all over these fells and into neighbouring Mardale and Kentmere.

IN THE LAKE DISTRICT

If you are on these fells in the autumn, there's a good chance you may hear the annual rut. Like a cross between the deep mooing of cows and the rumble of distant trail bikes, this is the deep roaring made by the stags as they prepare for the mating season. Having congregated in single-sex herds for much of the year, they now go their separate ways and begin gathering their individual harems.

The deep bellow of the stag performs two functions. Firstly, the loudest, most frequent roar wins the females. Secondly, it forms part of the posturing used by a male to achieve dominance over other stags. Another element of this is the antler fight, during which the animals lock antlers and attempt to push each other away. The strongest secures a harem for mating.

The rut lasts about six weeks, during which time stags will patrol their harems, chasing off any rival stags that come near and ensuring their hinds are not tempted to stray. At the end of this period, the stags, often emaciated from such an energetic few weeks, leave the females. The young are born from mid-May to July.

> Eventually, you drop to a faint crossing of paths close to a tiny sheepfold. Turn right here. This path provides a quieter, more pleasant alternative to the main route to and from Boredale Hause. Turn right at a junction with a stonier path. Later, just after passing a bench, you will be joined by a path coming in from the left. Turn left at the T-junction above the cottages and then drop to the large gate. Once through this, turn right. The rough track passes some cottages on your right. Turn left between the buildings at Side Farm and follow the farm track to the road.
>
> To return to Glenridding, you must now turn right. There is a footpath beside the road all the way, but you will need to cross and recross on several occasions, passing St Patrick's Church along the way. If you have parked at the pier itself, you should go through a small gate in the

fence immediately after St Patrick's Boat Landing. This gives access to a lakeside path that leads to the car park.

The **Ullswater Navigation and Transit Company Limited** started operating services in 1859, carrying mail, provisions and passengers around the lake. Two 19th-century 'steamers' still operate on the lake – the Raven and the Lady of The Lake – although both were converted to diesel in the 1930s. Another three boats were added to the fleet this century. ◆

Romans in Cumbria

The Roman legions first entered the far north-west of England in about 71AD, when Petillius Cerialis began to crush the Brigantes, the Celtic people who dominated the region at the time. Agricola then managed to push north from Chester to Carlisle in 78AD and placed garrisons between the Solway Firth and the River Tyne.

Although there is little trace of three centuries of Roman rule in local place-names or the Cumbrian dialect, the impression left upon the landscape by the occupation is clear to see. From around 120AD, a system of roads was built, including High Street, the highest Roman road in the country, which runs for 25 miles across the eastern fells from the Roman fort Brocavum at Brougham, near Penrith to Galava. Cumbria is also dotted with the remains of forts, milecastles, marching camps, bath-houses and, of course, the magnificent Hadrian's Wall. Created on the orders of the Emperor Hadrian, work on the wall began in 122AD. It ran from Bowness-on-Solway to Wallsend on the Tyne estuary.

IN THE LAKE DISTRICT

10
GUMMER'S HOW

Start/Finish: Forestry Commission Gummer's How car park on Fell Foot Brow at southern end of Windermere (SD389876)
Distance: 2.7km (1¾ miles)
Height gain: 122m (400ft)
Type of walk: Clear path, rocky in places, on ascent; return uses less well trodden trail
Refreshments: The nearest pub is the Masons Arms near Cartmel Fell

*This short walk takes you to one of the most popular viewpoints in the whole of the National Park. Even though the top of **Gummer's How** is only 321m above sea level, it commands some excellent views – of the high Lakeland fells to the north, to the Howgills and the Pennines in the east and out across Morecambe Bay to the south. The ascent route is well-trodden, although it is rocky in places. The descent, on the other hand, uses a quieter, mostly grassy path.*

TURN RIGHT OUT OF THE CAR PARK and walk up the road. After about 120 metres, go through the gate on the left. A good path skirts the base of a conifer-covered slope. As the trees begin to thin out, ignore a faint path off to the right – this is the route you will use on your descent towards the end of the walk. The main path soon begins to climb, a series of steps easing the ascent. At the base of Gummer's How proper, having left most of the trees behind, you come to a fence corner. As the fence swings right, bear left to climb a steep and rocky path. At

SHORT WALKS

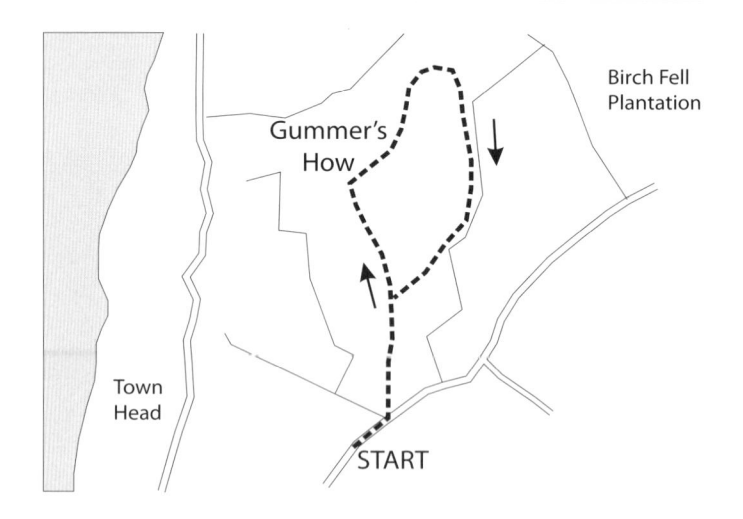

the top of the first rise, you get a spectacular view of the Coniston fells to the NW. Bear right to clamber up through more rocky outcrops. Eventually, you reach the trig pillar from where you have far-reaching views in all directions.

Take the faint path heading slightly E of N across the top of the fell. Before long, this begins to descend at an easy angle. After about 300 metres, bear right (NE) at a fork. The path drops into a dip and then swings right (S). You soon have a fenced plantation on your left. Keep close to this as you skirt the base of Gummer's How's eastern slopes.

When the fence bends sharp left, the path veers away from the forest slightly. With good views to the SW, you drop back down to the main path, along which you turn left. Turn right at the road to return to the car park. ◆

IN THE LAKE DISTRICT

11

GRIZEDALE FOREST AND HAWKSHEAD

Start/Finish: Moor Top car park (Pay and Display)
in Grizedale Forest (SD342965)
Distance: 7.1km (4½ miles)
Height gain: 219m (718ft)
Type of walk: Forest tracks; farm paths; some road walking
Refreshments: Choice of cafés, pubs and
restaurants in Hawkshead

*A stroll across a tiny corner of the immense **Grizedale Forest** is followed by a walk along farm paths through lovely, rolling countryside in the South Lakes. The route drops down into **Hawkshead** where you can get refreshments from any one of a large number of pubs and cafés before heading out to Howe Farm near Esthwaite Water and then climbing back up to Hawkshead Moor. Apart from a brief section after leaving the forest, all the paths are well signposted and easy to follow. There are a few short, easy climbs along the way, the hardest of which comes near the end of the walk.*

AS YOU HEAD INTO THE FOREST, the wide forest road splits just beyond the wooden barrier. Bear right – towards Hawkshead. When you reach a three-way split, take the middle option – a narrower track heading gently uphill. Rejoining the forest road, turn right and then, almost immediately, right again. At almost 250 metres above sea level, this is the highest point on the walk. After passing a small pool in the trees to your left, you

Short Walks

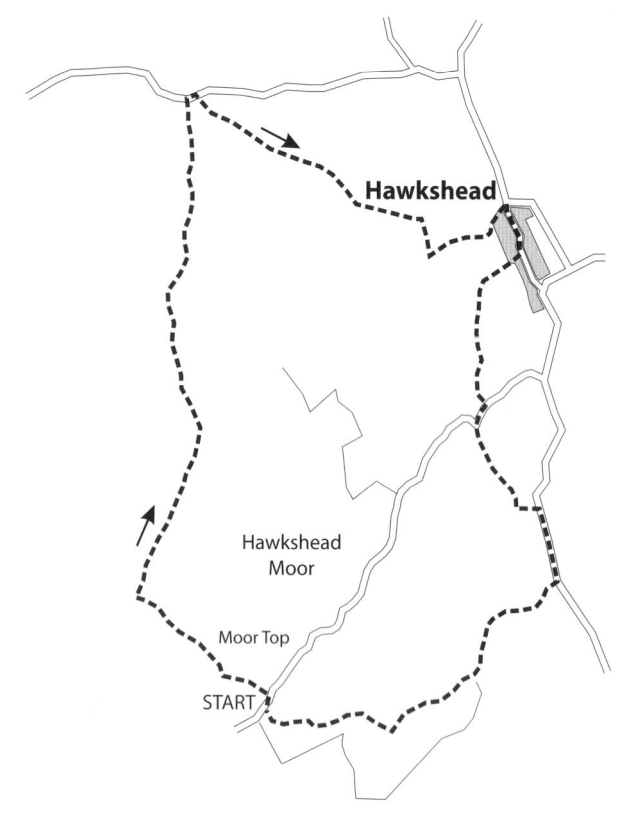

join a wider track. Ignore a path to the right here. At the next junction, go straight across, continuing in the same direction on a narrow path through the trees.

Like much of this area, the woods around Grizedale used to belong to the wealthy monks of Furness Abbey, and, in the early 16th century, it became a deer park. The Forestry Commission has owned the land since the 1930s.

IN THE LAKE DISTRICT

The forests here are home to a great variety of wildlife, including one or two rare British species. There have been reported sightings, for example, of the elusive pine marten. Due partly to hunting, poisoning and loss of habitat, this weasel-like mammal had become extinct throughout much of Britain by the early part of the 20th century. Small populations are thought to have survived in areas of northern England and Wales, with larger populations in parts of the Scottish Highlands where a recovery is now under way. Adults are about the size of a small domestic cat and have long tails. They have brown fur and a creamy 'bib' on the throat and chest.

The southern part of Grizedale Forest is also home to a tiny population of dormice. With the loss of semi-natural woodland and the decline in coppicing over the last 100 years or so, the dormouse has practically disappeared from northern England. Of course, it spends a huge amount of its life sleeping, so, as with the pine marten, you'd be extremely lucky to see one. The best time of day to spot one is dusk in late summer, just as they emerge to forage for food. Fruit, berries and hazel-nuts are their favourite meals.

A sure sign that dormice are living in the area is the proliferation on the ground of hazel-nuts with smoothly chiselled, circular holes in them. Other small mammals, such as mice and voles, create corrugated edges around the inside of the hole. Not so the dormouse, which uses its lower incisors to work away at the shell as the nut is rotated.

> Leave the confines of the forest via a small gate in the boundary fence, and follow an indistinct path beside the beck. When you reach what looks like a junction of paths, bear left across the beck and through a kissing-gate. There is no path on the ground now, but keep heading N and you will soon see a marker post just to the left of a pair of trees straight ahead. Continue N from here, aiming just to the left of a power line pole. When you reach a rough farm track, turn right and then left through a kissing-gate. Continue N, towards the wall on your right, where you will pick up a narrow path leading to the road.

SHORT WALKS

> Go through the wooden gate and then through the kissing-gate on your immediate right – towards Hawkshead. The path soon crosses a concrete farm track and drops to a kissing-gate. It crosses a couple of small footbridges and then swings left to follow the beck downstream for a short while. Follow the fence until it kinks left. Now go through the awkward kissing-gate straight ahead to walk with a fence on your right. Beyond the next kissing-gate, follow the fence on your left down to a surfaced lane, along which you turn left.
>
> At the bottom of Vicarage Lane in Hawkshead, turn right to pass to the right of the Co-op, then head diagonally across the square to walk with the Market Hall Meeting Room on your left. Enter the churchyard and, as you pass the church on your left, swing right to walk below a burial area on a small hill.

St Micheal and All Angels Church was built in the 15th century, although there have been improvements and additions since then.

Close to the church is **Hawkshead's old grammar school**, a free school that was established in 1585 by Edwin Sandys, of nearby Esthwaite Hall. Sandys spent some time as a prisoner in the Tower of London under Mary Tudor, but then became Archbishop of York under Elizabeth I. The school's most famous pupil was William Wordsworth.

The young poet boarded with Ann Tyson while he was at the school, first in a beautiful 16th-century cottage in the middle of the village and then out at Colthouse. Having lost his mother a few years earlier, Wordsworth adored the kind and maternal Mrs Tyson and described her in *The Prelude* as "my old Dame, so motherly and good..."

> Leave the church grounds and head towards another gate, beyond which you turn left – towards Roger Ground. A well-defined trail leads through a series of kissing-gates to a minor road, along which you turn right. Walk uphill for 100 metres. When the road bends sharp right, turn

IN THE LAKE DISTRICT

> left along a narrow lane – towards Howe Farm. Keep to the lane, even when it seems like you're heading down someone's private drive. When you reach a gate with a 'private' sign on it, cross the small bridge to the right and follow the fence on your left to the farm. When you reach the buildings, go through the gate on the left and follow the path round to the right to reach the farm track. Turn left and then right along the road.

The lake on the left is **Esthwaite Water**, a relatively shallow body of water that is about 2.5km (1½ miles) long and just a few hundred metres wide. It is home to the largest trout fishery in the north-west of England and, as such, is one of the most popular fishing spots in the area.

It is hoped that salmon will one day return to the lake. The fish cages at Hawkshead Trout Farm have been removed and the fishery is moving from stocking rainbow trout to native brown trout in a bid to return the lake to a more natural state. Improved water quality and the long-term removal of non-indigenous species will ultimately allow the removal of the fish screen on Cunsey Beck, which currently prevents the movement of rainbow trout downstream to Windermere. This in turn will enable salmon to migrate through Esthwaite Water to their natural spawning grounds in the headwaters above the lake.

> Walk along the road for 300 metres and then turn right along the second of two tracks running parallel with each other. The track soon swings left to pass to the right of a white cottage and then goes through a large gate – this time it really does enter someone's front yard. Go through the gate to the left of the building and then walk up the rough track beside the beck.
>
> After leaving the wooded area, follow the clearly waymarked trail, which swings left to climb the grassy hillside. Twisting and turning all the way, the path eventually leads up to some buildings. Follow the wide vehicle track all the way to the road. Turn right and the parking area is on the left. ♦

SHORT WALKS

12

HAWKSHEAD TO NEAR SAWREY VIA LATTERBARROW

Start: Queen's Head Inn, Hawkshead (SD352981)
Finish: Near Sawrey (SD370956)
Distance: 7.6km (4¾ miles)
Height gain: 268m (880ft)
Type of walk: Forest tracks; grassy hill path; some road walking
Refreshments: Choice of cafés, pubs and restaurants in Hawkshead; Tower Bank Arms in Near Sawrey

*This is Beatrix Potter country and it's hard to escape from references to this famous writer and illustrator of children's book as you wander down the secret alleyways and cobbled yards of **Hawkshead**, past lonely tarns sparkling in hidden bowls in the hills and up to one of the best viewpoints in this part of the Lake District. This is the landscape that inspired both her art and her farming – and led her to become a key figure in the early development of the National Trust.*

*The highest point on the walk is little **Latterbarrow**. At a mere 244 metres, this little bump on the landscape is barely worthy of the title 'fell', but it makes a grand place to visit on a clear day. You're unlikely to have the summit to yourself – it's a popular walk from busy Hawkshead – but don't let that spoil your enjoyment as you slowly turn 360 degrees at the top to take in your magnificent surroundings.*

WITH YOUR BACK TO THE QUEEN'S HEAD INN, turn right and you will soon see the Beatrix Potter Gallery on your

> right. Just after the Red Lion, turn right. Towards the end of this lane, swing left to go through a small gate. Cross the road and go down the track opposite. After the beck, turn left. Follow the surfaced path to a small gate and then continue in the same direction to another gate. Beyond this, bear left. Turn left along a rough track and then right, through a kissing-gate. Turn right along Loanthwaite Lane.
>
> At the T-junction, turn left and then right through a signposted gate. When the clear path forks, bear left to climb more steeply to the tall column on top of Latterbarrow. With no other high ground nearby, the views in all directions are far-reaching.

The woods that you are about to enter are said to be haunted by a hooded figure, possibly the ghost of a monk. The story goes back a long, long time – to when, one stormy night, the ferrymen of Windermere heard an eerie voice summoning them from the western shores. Most chose to ignore the call, but one young oarsman set off to collect his fare. He returned several hours later, ashen-faced and struck dumb. What had happened to him out there on the lake? What had he seen? His colleagues never found out for he soon developed a fever and, within days, was dead.

The voice continued to call out from the Claife Heights on wild nights, but the ferrymen ignored it. Finally, a priest was called in to exorcise it – and the spirit was silenced.

There have been several theories to explain the origins of the so-called **Claife Crier**. In the book, *Ghosts and Legends of the Lake District*, J.A. Brooks suggests it may have been "an echo of one of the tragedies that occurred here in the 17th century". In 1635 and again in 1681, two boats sank on Windermere, drowning all onboard. In the first accident, 47 wedding guests were killed on their way home from the ceremony. Maybe it was one of these long-lost revellers that the young ferrymen saw?

Local legend has it that the calls came from the ghost of a monk from Furness Abbey who was prevented from marrying the woman he loved by

Short Walks

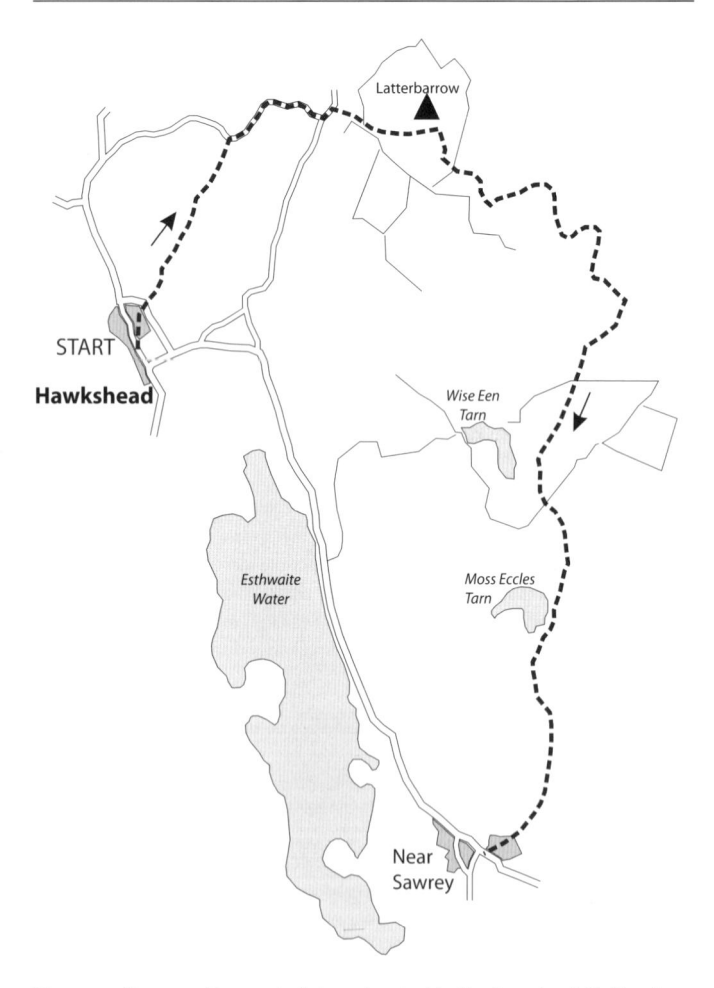

his monastic vows. Tormented, he retreated to the forests of Claife where he died of grief.

IN THE LAKE DISTRICT

> From the top, follow the wide track (S) through the bracken. Cross the stile and follow the track through the woods. Beyond a gap in a wall, keep to the track as it swings right and then left. At the next wall corner, it swings right again for a few metres and then crosses a gap in a wall. Crossing an open area, it then follows a wall back up to the forest proper. Turn left at the junction and then right at the next crossing of paths – towards Far Sawrey. Take the next path on your right. This quickly joins a wider track.
>
> Beyond the next gate, you cross open ground. The path briefly disappears, but there are waymarkers to guide you back on to a clear path passing between two tarns – the larger of the two, on your right, is called Wise Een Tarn. About 800 metres beyond these, you reach Moss Eccles Tarn.

Beatrix Potter bought **Moss Eccles Tarn** in 1913. She and her husband William Heelis kept a boat on the tarn and spent many happy summer evenings here – he fishing, she sketching. They also planted one red water lily and one white water lily. It's now a Site of Special Scientific Interest with a range of aquatic plants as well as damselflies and dragonflies.

> After a couple more gates, bear right at a clear, signposted fork in the track. When you reach the village, the bus stops are up to your left, but take some time to explore the tiny village before heading back to Hawkshead.

It was in Near Sawrey that Potter bought her first farm – **Hill Top** in 1905. Over the next eight years, she drew inspiration from the area and at least seven of her books are set on the farm or in the countryside surrounding it. Now owned by the National Trust, to which Beatrix bequeathed 13 farms and about 4,000 acres on her death in 1943, it is open to the public. Other buildings in the village featured in her stories too, including the Tower Bank Arms, which she painted in *The Tale of Jemima Puddle-Duck*. ◆

SHORT WALKS

13

TARN HOWS
AND MONK CONISTON

Start/Finish: Lake District National Park's Monk Coniston pay and display car park at the northern end of Coniston Water (SD316978)
Distance: 7.6km (4¾ miles)
Height gain: 245m (803ft)
Type of walk: Forest tracks; tarn path; quiet road; farm paths
Refreshments: Choice of cafés, pubs and restaurants in nearby Coniston

Despite being man-made, Tarn Hows is one of the most popular beauty spots in the whole of the Lake District. And it is well worth a visit, especially if you come at it from the south. This walk does exactly that, starting from the northern end of Coniston Water, passing through the lovely Monk Coniston arboretum and then gently climbing good tracks through attractive woodland until you are standing looking down on this picturesque Victorian creation. Having completed a circuit of Tarn Hows, the route then returns via a quiet road and pleasant farm paths.

FROM THE PARKING AREA, WALK TO THE ROAD, cross straight over and go through the gate opposite. A grassy path heads gently uphill through National Trust land. Go through the small gate in the metal railings and follow the gravel path round to the right, up through the arboretum. At a junction close to the walled garden, go through the gate in the wall. Continue straight ahead to a T-junction of paths and then turn left to exit the gardens via a tall metal gate. Head downhill, crossing straight over a track, and then keep right – along a track through the trees, signposted Tarn Hows.

The **arboretum** here was planted by James Garth Marshall, a Leeds industrialist who had made his money from the flax-spinning industry. He bought the 700-acre Monk Coniston estate from the Knott family in 1835. The original building on the site of the current hall is said to have been constructed by the monks of Furness Abbey in the 13th century.

Cross the minor road and head straight up the trail climbing gently through the woods. Soon after crossing a narrow, dam-like footbridge, the track climbs some steps to a T-junction. Turn right along the permitted bridleway. Turn left at the next T-junction, along a permitted cycleway. Bear right at a fork in the track, and then turn left at a path junction close to the edge of the trees.

You soon reach a minor road looking down over Tarn Hows. Cross straight over – into the disabled parking area and then along the surfaced track. Take the next track on your left, which has a barrier across it. Once through the gate at the bottom, bear right along the clear track to continue your circuit of Tarn Hows. The constructed path goes all the way around it.

With plans based on the ideas of the 'Picturesque' that were popular at the time, James Marshall created **Tarn Hows** by damming one of the original three tiny tarns on the site to create the single body of water that exists today. He also planted the conifer plantations that surround it, intending both to frame and reveal views of his new creation.

Beyond the gate at the south-western edge of the water, take the middle of the three paths. Just after you join a path coming in from the right, bear right at a fork. Turn right along the road, crossing a cattle grid just beyond the main car park. The road winds its way down the hillside with superb views across to Wetherlam on the other side of the valley.

SHORT WALKS

Tom Heights

Tarn Hows

Tarn Hows Wood

Monk Coniston

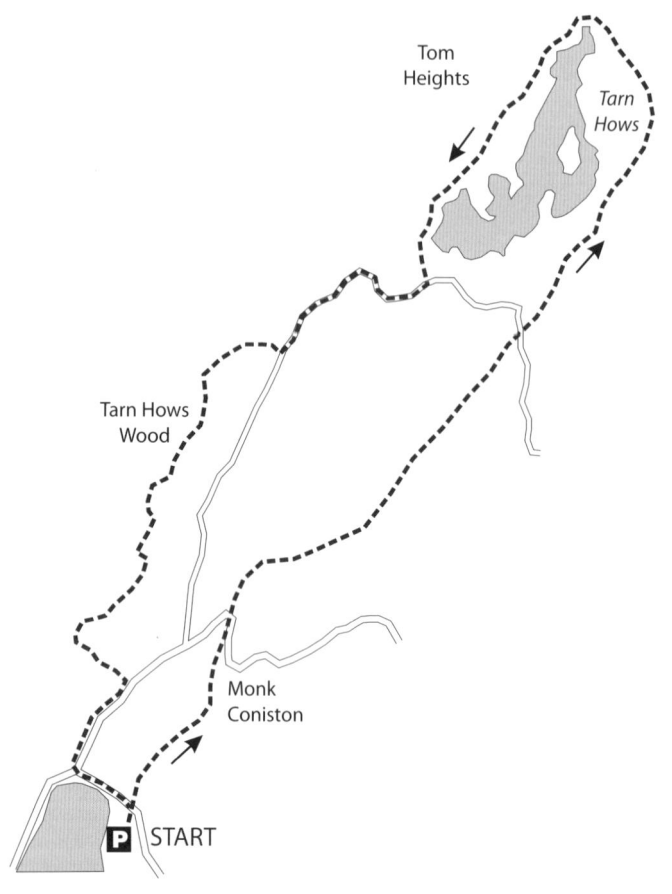

START

Turn right, through a kissing-gate and along a clear track, towards Low Yewdale. As the track swings sharp right to drop to a cottage, go through the large gate on your left. The faint grassy path, muddy in places, heads away from the wall in a SSW direction. Beyond the first field, it

> goes through a gate and then keeps fairly close to some woods on the right. When the fence on the right swings away, the path swings left. Just a few metres beyond the next gate/stile, the path – indistinct at this point – swings sharp left to pass to the left of a group of large trees.

As you descend, with Coniston Water directly ahead, you will soon be able to see **Monk Coniston** below to the left. In 1926, as the Marshall family fortunes declined, the house and gardens were sold to John Perry Bradshaw. Beatrix Potter bought the rest of the estate, including all the farmland and Tarn Hows, in 1930. Almost immediately, she sold half at cost price to the National Trust; and the other half passed to the charity after her death in 1943. The National Trust purchased the hall and gardens in 1945, re-uniting the estate once more.

> Beyond the gate at the bottom of the path, turn left along the rough track, soon passing Boon Crag Farm. Turn right at the road and then, almost immediately, go through the gap on your right to pick up a permitted bridleway. This runs parallel with the road all the way to Coniston, but you follow it only until it approaches the lakeshore. When it does so, go through the gap in the hedge on your left and take the road turning on the left, towards Brantwood. The car park is about 200 metres along this road on your right.

Brantwood was the home of the great Victorian intellectual **John Ruskin**. He was born in London in 1819, and first visited the Lake District when he was five years old. He once said that the "first thing I remember as an event in life was being taken by my nurse to the brow of Friar's Crag on Derwentwater". It was, he continued, "the creation of the world for me". He made his home on the shores of Coniston Water in 1872 and lived there until he died in 1900.

One of the most influential thinkers of his age, he wrote more than 250 works on subjects as diverse as literary criticism, social theory, the history of art, mythology, ornithology and pollution. Containing a strong desire

Short Walks

to improve conditions for the poor, his ideas had a profound effect on the early development of the Labour Party in Britain. His many fans included Marcel Proust and Mahatma Gandhi, who translated Ruskin's *Unto This Last*, a damning critique of capitalist economics, into Gujarati. Leo Tolstoy described him as "one of the most remarkable men, not only of England and of our own time, but of all countries and all times". ◆

Gondola

A pleasant way to see Coniston Water is from the National Trust's restored steam yacht, Gondola. The original Gondola was first launched in 1859 by Sir James Ramsden, a director of the Furness Railway Company. She carried tourists up and down the length of the lake until 1936, when she was decommissioned. She then became a houseboat until a storm ripped her from her moorings and beached her in the early 1960s. She was finally restored and relaunched in 1980.

Today, Gondola carries passengers between Coniston Pier and the Brantwood and Monk Coniston jetties, a round trip of about 45 minutes. There are also occasional 90-minute cruises along the full length of Coniston Water, during which visitors learn about some of the most famous people associated with Coniston – John Ruskin, Donald Campbell, Arthur Ransome et al.

IN THE LAKE DISTRICT

14

WHITBARROW

Start/Finish: There is parking close to Witherslack Hall School (SD437859). If approaching the school from the south, turn right along a rough track just in front of its entrance. There is room for a few cars here
Distance: 8.9km (5½ miles)
Height gain: 255m (835ft)
Type of walk: Woodland trails; steep, stony ascent; good paths on grassy fell
Refreshments: The Derby Arms Hotel, Witherslack

Walkers don't normally associate the Lake District with limestone, but the south of the National Park is home to several small hills characterised by the clints and grikes of limestone pavement. **Whitbarrow** *is one of these, rising to a high point of 215m at Lord's Seat. The open grasslands on the ridge top, part of a National Nature Reserve, are home to juniper, wildflowers and rare butterflies. They also provide magnificent views of the south Cumbrian estuaries as they open out into Morecambe Bay. The paths are generally good, although the short climb up Bell Rake is quite steep and rough.*

WALK ALONG THE ROUGH, WIDE TRACK to the right of the start of Witherslack Hall School's driveway. Once through the gate at the end, take the track on the left, heading almost straight towards Chapel Head Scar, where peregrines often nest. Bear left at the next fork to head through a kissing-gate and into the attractive woodland.

Keep to the clear, waymarked track, which is a permissive

Short Walks

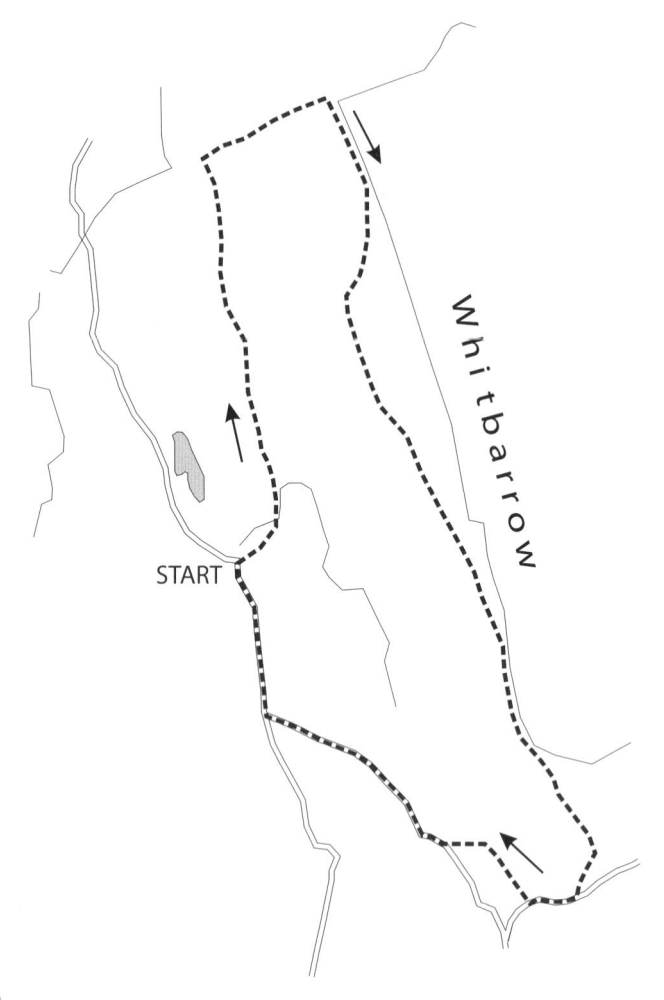

route, and don't be tempted by any paths off until, about
50 metres back from a wall, you reach a signposted

junction of paths. Turn right here – signposted Bell Rake and Whitbarrow. The path zigzags up through the trees and through a small gate to enter the Hervey Memorial Reserve. One more short pull, on loose rock at first, brings you out on to the open fell near the remains of an old mine.

Keep close to the wall on your left until it starts to drop to a ladder stile in the wall corner. Don't descend to the stile; instead, turn right (SSE) along a faint path, climbing gently through sparse woodland. The start of the path is marked by a cairn. It follows the line of the wall on your left at first and then swings away to cross an area of limestone pavement on its way up to Lord's Seat, the highest point on the fell.

The top is marked by a large cairn dedicated to Canon Hervey, the founder of the Lake District Naturalists' Trust. From here, you can look south into Morecambe Bay; the Howgills and the Pennines are clearly visible to the west; and, to the north, the high Lake District fells dominate the scene.

Whitbarrow, meaning White Hill, is an area of carboniferous limestone, laid down about 350 million years ago. More than half the fell is a National Nature Reserve, managed by the Cumbria Wildlife Trust and the Forestry Commission. The reserve includes some of Britain's 2,600 hectares of limestone pavement as well as ancient ash-hazel and yew woodland and a significant area of juniper scrub.

Limestone pavement is the result of the interplay of the soluble nature of the rock and the work of glaciers. About 2.6 million years ago the Earth began to cool, resulting in the formation of glaciers that covered huge areas of land with massive ice sheets. Although this tends to be called the 'Ice Age', within this Ice Age there were cold periods (glacials) and warmer periods (inter-glacials) when forests thrived.

The creation of limestone pavement began as the glaciers of the last cold period, which ended about 10,000 years ago, scoured the rock and ice, fracturing it along existing horizontal lines of weakness known as bedding planes. Over time water has been exploiting the bedding planes and other cracks in the limestone, slowly eroding and dissolving the rock. This has created the fascinating pattern of blocks (clints) and fissures (grikes) that we see today. Look into these sheltered grikes on Whitbarrow and you'll see ferns such as hart's tongue and wildflowers such as hoary rockrose and wood sorrel. Juniper, used to flavour gin, is also abundant on the ridge.

> From the summit, you can see the continuing path stretching into the distance (SSE) – along the top of the limestone ridge. Striding out with ease, you get good views ahead, particularly of the Kent Estuary. After a while, the path swings left to pass under a low, but interesting limestone scar. After crossing a stile in a wall, keep straight ahead. As you approach the southern end of Whitbarrow, you can see the River Kent meandering its way towards Morecambe Bay and the Irish Sea.

While much of the woodland on Whitbarrow's lower slopes is managed by coppicing to encourage butterfly-friendly plants such as violet, primrose and hairy dog violet, the summit area is grazed by cattle under an organic system. Restoration of this grassland, which used to be covered by pine woodland, is helping to preserve other rare plant communities and herb-rich foliage that is home to two of the UK's most endangered species of butterfly – the high brown fritillary and the pearl-bordered fritillary.

The butterflies can be seen both on the grassy summit and in woodland clearings in the summer. The smaller, pearl-bordered variety, tends to fly close to the ground, stopping regularly to feed on flowers. The more powerful high brown is a faster mover.

The larvae hatch in early spring and spend long periods basking in short, sparse vegetation. The temperatures here can be several degrees higher than in grassy areas, allowing the larvae to develop quickly in otherwise cool weather.

> The path soon starts descending through the trees. It goes through a gate in a wall and then swings left,

back over the wall almost straightaway. Keep to the waymarked route – ignoring any other paths – until you reach a T-junction with a wider path. Turn right here, heading down through the woods. Turn right when you reach a wide track. When this swings left, turn right along a footpath – towards Beck Head.

Go through a stile in a wall and then keep close to the wall on your left to reach a gate. Once through this, keep going in the same direction – apparently through someone's garden – until you reach a large wooden gate. Just beyond this is a minor road. Turn left if you want to see where the beck emerges from beneath a limestone scar; but the main route goes right. The road soon becomes a rough track and you pass the last of the buildings of Beck Head on your left. Ignore the path off to your right in a short while; keep to the wide bridleway. Turn right at the road and return to the school's entrance. ◆

SHORT WALKS

15
WALLOWBARROW

Start/Finish: Small parking area near the church in Seathwaite,
Duddon Valley (SD229961)
Distance: 6.8km (4¼ miles)
Height gain: 323m (1,060ft)
Type of walk: Mostly good paths and tracks,
but short pathless section on felltop
Refreshments: Newfield Inn, Seathwaite

Wallowbarrow is a mere 292m above sea level and yet it commands an excellent view of the beautiful Duddon Valley. Forsaken by those who seek out the higher summits, its rocky top is well worth exploring. This route completes a circuit of the fell using a combination of good paths and tracks on its western side. Some walkers may choose to omit the short climb to the summit, reducing the total route by a few hundred metres and cutting out a small amount of ascent, but they're missing out! The eastern side of the circuit follows the River Duddon through an impressive gorge. Here, at the base of Wallowbarrow Crag, with peregrines nesting on high ledges overhead, the river's crystal clear waters have to negotiate the huge boulders that have tumbled down the slope. Beautiful, deep, blue pools alternate with fast-moving rapids as you follow the river downstream.

FROM THE PARKING AREA, TURN RIGHT along the road, and, in about 30 metres, take the signposted footpath on your right. This goes through an awkward squeeze stile and then follows the river bank for a short while. After crossing the footbridge, the path heads upstream

IN THE LAKE DISTRICT

through the trees for a short while and then swings away from the beck. Having crossed the River Duddon via a humpback bridge, take the path heading away from the water, just to the left of the National Trust signpost. Once through the next gate, you will see a gate in a fence corner straight ahead; the path you want is at the top of the short slope to the right of this. Following the line of the wall/fence on your right, go through two gates to enter the farmyard at High Wallowbarrow.

Go through the gate to the right of the farmhouse. This provides access to a bridleway that soon begins to climb beside a beck. The rough track zigzags its way uphill beneath what, from below, seem like huge, towering crags.

As the gradient begins to ease and the rocky slopes on your right give way to grass, strike off right (ESE) up a grassy gap between the crags. There is a faint path on the ground, but this becomes indistinct by the time you get your first view to the E – of the Coniston fells. Now head up on to the high ground to your right and clamber on to the rocky top of Wallowbarrow Crag itself.

Who can resist pausing here for a while to take in the wonderful setting? This tiny, craggy fell is surrounded on three sides by higher, rocky mountains, including Harter Fell to the N. But look to the SW and you see the long, green line of the Duddon Valley reaching out to the sea. You can't quite see where it enters Morecambe Bay because it swings S, but you can see the Black Combe and White Combe hills in the distance.

From the top, retrace your steps to the bridleway and turn right. Go through the gap in the wall and bear right. The Forestry Commission has planted native species of trees and shrubs in this area, including oak on the lower slopes, birch further up and, among the upper crags, juniper, rowan and holly. Please make sure you close any

73

Short Walks

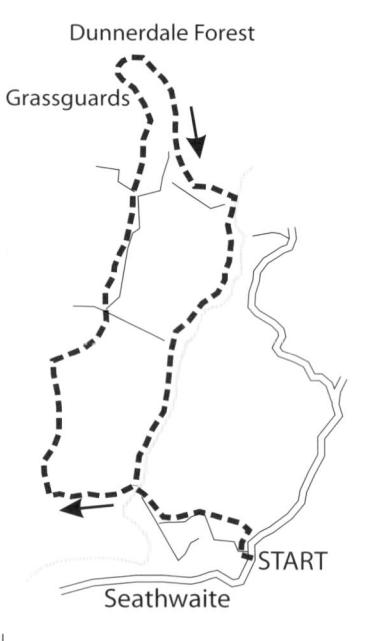

gates to prevent deer and sheep from getting in and damaging the saplings. The clear track eventually leads to Grassguards Farm.

Go through the gate on your left to follow a permissive path around the side of the buildings. When you come out on a track above Grassguards Gill, turn right and then cross the footbridge. Head down to the ford to your right and then turn left along the clear track. Almost immediately, turn right along a narrow path between a fence on your left and the beck on your right. After going through a gate, the descent becomes steeper and the path almost disappears beneath a layer of leaf litter. When you reach the River Duddon, turn right, soon crossing a footbridge over the tributary beck you have been following since the farm.

The path heads uphill briefly, following the fence on your right, before swinging left, to follow the Duddon downstream. The path becomes a little hard to identify as it climbs through the trees, but as long as you stay close to the fence on your right, you shouldn't go wrong. Stick with it even when it kinks right – even though you do seem to be increasing the distance between yourself and the river. Eventually, you drop closer to the water's edge and cross a stile. Before long, you cross a boulder slope at the base of Wallowbarrow Crag. Contrary to the warning signs you may have spotted earlier, this is

> unlikely to present you with any problems unless your attention to your footing is distracted. Simply take your time and enjoy this fascinating section of path.

Peregrines often nest on the crags of Wallowbarrow Gorge. These large and powerful falcons are said to be the fastest creatures on the planet, achieving speeds of up to 200mph in their hunting dives. They prey mostly on medium-sized birds, which they catch in mid-air. In flight, the bird can be identified by its long, pointed wings and relatively short tail. Its back is slate-grey and its breast is spotted. It has a black 'moustache', which contrasts with its pale face, and distinctive yellow feet. Peregrines mate for life and return to the same nesting spot each year, building a 'scrape' on crag or cliff ledges.

Peregrine numbers fell to an all-time low in the first half of the 20th century. They were killed by gamekeepers and landowners, and were a target for egg collectors, but better legal protection and control of pesticides – which indirectly poisoned the birds – have helped the population to recover considerably since the 1960s.

> Having crossed a wall, you will soon recognise the humpback bridge you crossed at the start of the walk. Turn left to cross it and retrace your steps to the parking area. ◆

SHORT WALKS

16
DEVOKE WATER

Start/Finish: The walk starts from the Stanley Ghyll road turning on the Birker Fell road, about 4.3km (2¾ miles) SE of the King George IV pub in Eskdale (SD170977)
Distance: 6.9km (4¼ miles)
Total ascent: 346m (1,134ft)
Type of walk: Good track to start, but mostly pathless, grassy fells after that. Many boggy patches
Refreshments: King George IV pub in Eskdale

*The largest tarn in the Lake District, **Devoke Water** is situated on lonely moorland to the south of Eskdale. This walk explores the high ground to the south and north of the tarn, visiting White Pike (442m), Water Crag (305m) and Rough Crag (319m). The heights may seem modest, but don't underestimate these little hills; they are boggy, paths are few and far between, and there is a serious chance of getting lost in misty conditions. With these considerations in mind, if you're competent with map and compass, you've got a good pair of boots on your feet and the weather's set fair, you're in for a cracking half-day. The views are dominated, to the north-east, by England's highest and most dramatic mountains and, to the west, by the Irish Sea.*

HEAD ALONG THE ROUGH TRACK opposite the Stanley Ghyll turning – towards Devoke Water. Before long, you will see the dark waters of the tarn ahead of you. The solid track ends close to the boathouse. Now turn left along the very rough, wet track beside the tarn. You quickly cross a beck, barely discernible among all this

IN THE LAKE DISTRICT

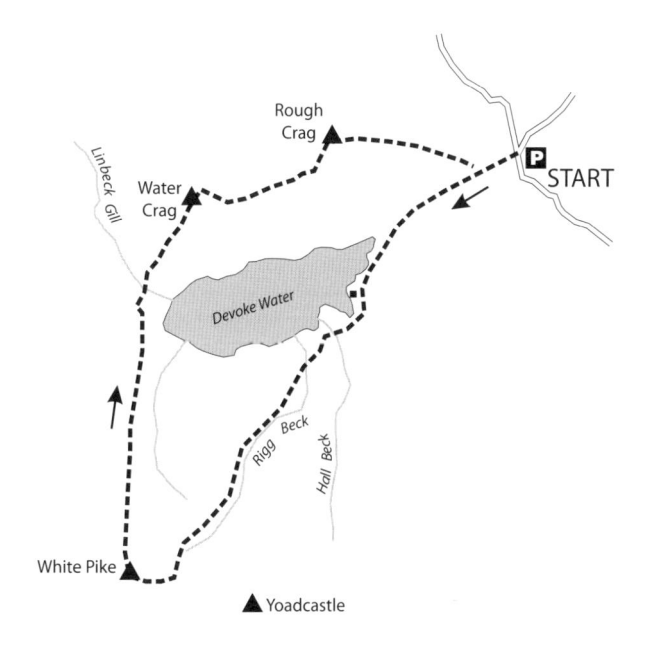

wet stuff, and, about 50 metres beyond that, you need to strike off left (SSW).

There is no path to speak of at first, although you should pick up a faint trail beyond the next beck in less than 100 metres. After another 300 metres of moderate ascent, you ford a third, wider stream, known as Rigg Beck. The trail continues SW for a short while, but then all but disappears. Continue following Rigg Beck upstream and, once you're beyond a couple of boggy areas, you will eventually pick up a clear path through the grass again. As the climb eases and the ground to your left becomes rockier, bear left at an indistinct fork in the path (SWW, veering SW). As you draw level with the boggy head of Rigg Beck over to the left, keep to the clearest route as the grassy path swings slightly left to climb a little more steeply. Reaching the top of the ridge, you cross a faint path, but you need to keep going a little further yet – until you get your first view W, straight out over the Irish Sea. Now turn right along a clear path along the edge of the fell. This climbs easily to the cairn marking the top of White Pike. From here you get a magnificent view of the coast and of the River Esk as it widens out to form the sandy estuary at Ravenglass.

Unfortunately, the clear path ends here and you now have to rely on your reading of both the map and the terrain to get you down to the western end of Devoke Water, which lies NNE of White Pike. There is no right or wrong way of doing this, and no one path that will take you all the way to the water's edge, but you may briefly pick up occasional trails and sheeptrods along the way that will make the going just that little bit easier.

If you go a little beyond the summit cairn, keeping it on your left, the ground drops away quite suddenly to the N and you can see – roughly – what lies between you and Devoke Water. Carefully pick your way down the steep ground in front of you, winding your way between the rocks. Beyond this, the descent is mostly on grass and relatively straightforward, but keep a careful eye on both your footing and your direction (generally NNE from the summit cairn) – don't be distracted by the fantastic panorama of mountains above Eskdale that is now laid out ahead of you. As you lose height, keep to the left of boggy ground marking the start of becks feeding into the tarn, although, eventually, it becomes impossible to avoid getting your feet wet.

After crossing a flat, particularly damp area, you reach a muddy track about 100 metres back from the tarn. Turn left and then, after another very boggy patch in a few metres, turn right along a faint path running parallel with the western edge of Devoke Water. Keep right at any forks to skirt the edge of the bracken. The trail peters out as you encounter boggy ground next to the tarn's main outlet stream. Your next challenge is to ford this, and the best way of doing this is by using the line of rocks just back from the point where the beck begins to drop more dramatically.

Once across, pick up a faint path (NNE) that crosses yet more boggy ground and then climbs Water Crag. It's easy to lose sight of the main path as it swings right and the gradient eases; but at this point you must swing sharp left to reach the summit cairn and another wonderful view of both the mountains and the coast.

Drop down the eastern side of the fell to join a clear ridge path, along which you turn left. Ignore the faint path off to the right; keep to the clearest path, which makes its way across a flat and inevitably boggy area and then continues up on to Rough Crag.

From the cairn, the path off the fell can be picked up just to the right of the summit. It descends E, veering ESE. Ignore a path off to the left; you simply maintain either an E or ESE bearing at any forks.

Eventually, you drop back to the track you followed out to Devoke Water at the start of the walk. Turn left to return to the road.

The moorland around Devoke Water is dotted with evidence that **ancient people** once lived here. The climate was considerably warmer and calmer in the early to mid-Bronze Age, allowing man to move higher on to the fells; many Bronze Age sites in Cumbria are located at about 500 to 1,000ft above sea level.

Barnscar, just over a mile SW of Devoke Water, consists of substantial earthwork remains of both Bronze Age and Romano-British settlements, with enclosures, hut circles, field systems and cairns. Bronze Age pottery has been found here as well as an undated coin hoard. Aerial photographs have identified a stone avenue leading from Barnscar to Devoke Water. ♦

Coleridge's first climb

Coleridge's well-documented ascent of England's second highest mountain Scafell – and subsequent descent of Broad Stand – in August 1802 is regarded by many as the first recorded climb for leisure purposes. He climbed it from Wasdale via Broad Tongue, a relatively easy, crag-free route until near the top. In a letter to his friend Sara Hutchinson, he wrote of the summit: "O my God! What enormous mountains these are close by me... But o! What a look down under my feet! The frighfullest cove that might ever be seen. Huge perpendicular precipices... two huge pillars of lead-coloured stone – I am no measurer but their height and depth is terrible."

The map he was carrying fell a long way short of the high standards of today's Ordnance Survey maps, and it was a miracle that he lived to tell the tale of his subsequent descent from Scafell down the dreaded Broad Stand. Today, this remains an accident blackspot in the mountains. Wasdale Mountain Rescue Team records more call-outs to this steep, rocky and often slippery short-cut between Scafell and Scafell Pike than to any other location – and many of the accidents here have resulted in deaths.

IN THE LAKE DISTRICT

17

AROUND GOSFORTH

Start/Finish: Main public car park in Gosforth (NY067035)
Distance: 8.9km (5½ miles)
Height gain: 171m (560ft)
Type of walk: Quiet roads; rough tracks; farm paths; riverside path
Refreshments: Wheatsheaf Inn, Globe Inn, Lion and Lamb and Lakeland Habit café, all in Gosforth

Gosforth is a pleasant village of about 1,200 inhabitants that stands guard at the entrance to Wasdale. It is home to no fewer than three pubs, a couple of shops and a church which houses some fascinating Norse artefacts. Never straying too far from the village, this walk uses a combination of quiet roads, a riverside path and a good network of tracks and bridleways to explore the area. Despite the fact that the highest point on the walk is less than 200m above sea level, there are some surprisingly good and often far-reaching views to be had – of the mountains ringing Wasdale Head one minute; of the coast and the Irish Sea the next.

TURN LEFT OUT OF THE CAR PARK and walk through the village. Ignore the turning on your right to Santon Bridge and Eskdale in a short while; simply keep to the main road. Before long, you pass St Mary's Church on your left, which is well worth a visit.

The **churchyard of St Mary's** contains the tallest Norse cross in England, thought to have stood on the same spot for about 1,000 years. More than four metres tall, set in a stepped stone base and intricately carved with pagan and Norse symbols on one side and Christian motifs on the other, it is said to depict the victory of Christ over the heathen gods. Its meaning

SHORT WALKS

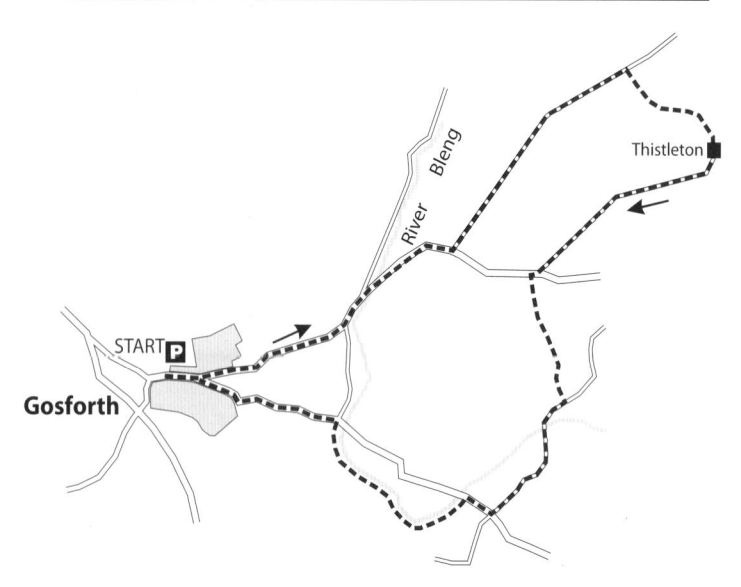

was lost until the 1880s when its carvings were linked to the Norse figure, Loki, found on a stone in the church at Kirkby Stephen.

The church also contains two 10th-century hogback tombstones carved with battle scenes. These are thought to have once covered the graves of Norse chieftains, but were then used in the foundations of the church's north wall in the 12th century. There were rediscovered there when the church underwent major rebuilding in 1896. Near to the church is one of the village's oldest buildings – **Gosforth Hall**, now a hotel. Built in 1658 for the Copley family, it is said that Robert Copley, who was careful with his money, built the upper storeys from the timbers of ships wrecked along the Irish Sea coast. The current owners claim that one of the rooms is haunted. They say that guests have woken in the dead of night to see a ghostly figure sitting beside the priests' hole, which was used as a hiding place for priests when Catholics in England were persecuted. Some guests have reported that the figure was either a monk or a friar wearing a religious habit.

IN THE LAKE DISTRICT

You eventually reach Wellington where you follow the main road round to the right, crossing the bridge over the River Bleng and continuing towards Wasdale. Having climbed for about 400 metres from the bridge, you will see a bench on the left, close to the brow of the hill. Swinging right, continue along the asphalt for another 150 metres.

Turn left along a lane known as Guards Lonning. With ever improving views of the mountains to the east, including Scafell, the track climbs steadily. The gradient eases as you pass Guards End, a home set about 100 metres back from the track. The next dwelling is Between Guards. About 100 metres beyond this, go through the large gate on your right – it has path markers on it. Cross the ladder stile in the wall on your right. Continue down the field with the wall on your left, soon crossing another ladder stile. Continue in the same direction for a short while and then swing left to pass through a wooden gate. Walk down the field with the wall on your right. Immediately ahead now are Whin Rigg and Illgill Head. After the next gate, the faint, grassy track veers away from the wall slightly and then swings right again, straight down the field, making for the farm at High Thistleton. Pass through one gate in a wall and then another to the left of the buildings.

Head down through the farmyard, keeping close to the main buildings on your right, and then leave via the access lane. Having swung round to the SW, the views of the fells have now been replaced by views out across the Irish Sea. This track eventually drops you on to the road. Cross straight over to pick up another track. When the main track swings right in a short while – towards the buildings at Bolton Head – keep left, crossing a stile beside a large gate to access a potentially muddy track. Having gone through a large gate, you reach a T-junction. Turn right along the wide track which soon crosses the River

Bleng via Hallbolton Bridge. The track passes beneath the buildings at Hall Bolton and then swings right.

When you reach the road, turn right. In 200 metres, just before the road crosses Bleng Bridge, go through the gate on the left to pick up a riverside path. Crossing several stiles along the way, keep close to the water's edge until you reach the next bridge. Go through the gate over to the left and then turn left along the road. Bear left at the junction in Gosforth, and the car park is now 250 metres ahead on the right. ◆

CUMBERLAND AND WESTMORLAND WRESTLING

Many of the annual agricultural shows held in the Lake District still host traditional Cumberland and Westmorland wrestling bouts. The origins of this unusual sport are unknown, but some think the Vikings brought it to England; others say it may have developed out of a longer-standing Celtic tradition. The wrestlers stand chest to chest, grasping each other around the body with their chins on their opponent's right shoulder. Once the umpire has started the contest by telling the men to 'tekk hod', they attempt to unbalance each other, or make their opponent lose their hold, using any method other than kicking. If any part of a wrestler's body touches the ground aside from his feet then he loses. Matches are decided by the best of three falls.

The traditional costume worn by the wrestlers can make these usually strong men look anything but butch – vests, white long johns, socks and, of course, those embroidered felt 'underpants' worn on the outside. But don't go along expecting the over-acting and prancing of modern American wrestling; this is a contest of skill, cunning and power, and it's taken very seriously by competitors.

IN THE LAKE DISTRICT

18

LOWESWATER CORPSE ROAD

Start/Finish: Maggie's Bridge car park near Loweswater (NY134210)
Distance: 8.9km (5½ miles)
Height gain: 271m (890ft)
Type of walk: Good tracks; quiet lanes; woodland path
Refreshments: The Kirkstile Inn, Loweswater

*This has to be one of the best low-level walks in the western Lakes. For relatively little effort and using clear, generally well-signposted bridleways, you get superb views of **Loweswater** and the fells nearby. There is a gentle climb near the beginning, but after that, you're on a wide, easy-to-follow track high above the lake. The return route is via quite lanes and a pleasant woodland path beside the lake, where you have a very good chance of seeing red squirrels.*

IGNORE THE PATH THAT HEADS WEST from the car park to Watergate Farm; instead, walk in the opposite direction – as if about to head back up the lane you have just driven – and then turn right after just a few metres. Go through the gate and, with Carling Knott straight ahead, follow the clear track up to High Nook Farm. Walk through the yard, passing the farmhouse on your left and then out through another gate.

Heading gently uphill with Highnook Beck down to your right, keep to the clear track next to the drystone wall on your left. Go through a gate in a wall and then, ignoring a path off to the left about 60 metres later, you begin to head slightly downhill. At the next, indistinct fork, bear

SHORT WALKS

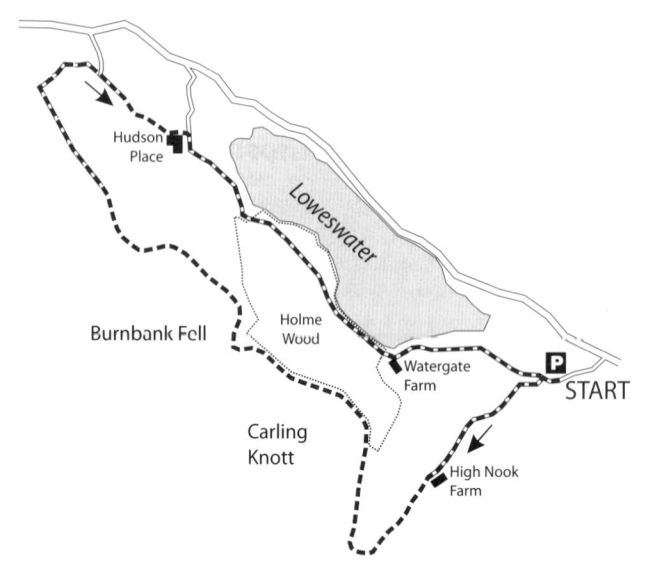

right and cross some soggy ground to drop down to a small wooden bridge across the beck.

Once across, the path swings right and climbs gently. You've now turned your back on the low-lying fells fells that occupy the ground to the south of Loweswater; facing you now are the more dramatic mountains on the other side of the Lorton Valley, including Whiteside and Grasmoor. After about 10 minutes of fairly gentle uphill work, the path levels off slightly and you reach the edge of a dark conifer plantation. A few minutes on the level is soon replaced by more uphill work. After the next gate, the views open out again: the Irish Sea can be seen far ahead, and, before long, you also catch glimpses of Loweswater through the trees. The lovely, grassy track drops down to cross Holme Beck and then continues its undulating way around the side of Burnbank Fell.

IN THE LAKE DISTRICT

From the beginning of the 13th century until the 17th century, when Loweswater was a chapel to St Bees Abbey, coffins would be carried on horseback along this bridleway to Lamplugh and then on to St Bees on the coast. This is one of many such 'corpse roads' in Cumbria, some of which inevitably have spooky stories associated with them, as we will see in Walk 22. Despite its morbid beginnings, it's a delightful path and it now has the added benefit of a well-placed bench just to the right of it, which affords some wonderful views down Loweswater and Crummock Water.

> Beyond the bench, climb gently to the first of several gates. Now heading downhill, go through another three gates and then, as the wide track swings sharp left, leave it by turning right over a ladder stile near a signpost.
>
> Heading towards 'Loweswater via Hudson Place', you soon begin to descend slowly, keeping close to the wall on the right. At a junction with a surfaced lane, turn right and then right again as you approach the grey cottages at Jenkinson Place. After crossing a stile by a gate, follow a faint path through the grass heading down to and through a gate. You then walk with a row of knarled trees and bushes on the left. Cross a double stile at another gate and head towards the buildings at Hudson Place. Just before the buildings, cross a stile beside the gate on your left. Now keep close to the fence on the right and follow it to the next gate.
>
> Once through, turn right along the lane, soon passing in front of the white-washed buildings of Hudson Place. Two gates mark the end of the lane just after the farmhouse; go through the left-hand one, which looks straight down on to shimmering Loweswater. At the bottom of this narrow path, cross the gate/stile to access the lakeshore track through Holme Woods.

The mixed woodland here is full of life compared with the dense conifers that you saw from the corpse road – birdlife is plentiful and you'd be unlucky not to see a red squirrel. Cumbria is one of the last strongholds of this native breed, which has been replaced in most of England and Wales by the grey squirrel, introduced from North America in 1876. There are estimated to be only 140,000 red squirrels left in the whole of Britain – most of which live in Scotland – compared with more than 2.5 million greys.

Partly because greys breed rapidly, with two litters a year, and are better able to survive a severe winter because of their extra body fat, they out-compete the reds, particularly in lowland deciduous woodland. They have been known to displace the native species completely within seven years of arrival in a wood. Red squirrels are also more susceptible to certain diseases, particularly the devastating squirrelpox virus, and find it less easy to adapt when hedgerows and woodland are destroyed.

Large conifer plantations provide red squirrels with a competitive advantage over greys. This is because, unlike in diverse broadleaf woodland, the only significant food source are the small seeds from conifer cones. With greys roughly twice the body weight of reds, these are insufficient for the invaders' needs.

> You eventually leave the woods via a gate. The track heads towards Watergate Farm and then swings sharp left just before the buildings. Follow it back to the car park. ◆

IN THE LAKE DISTRICT

19
BUTTERMERE

Start/Finish: Lake District National Park car park (Pay and Display) behind the Bridge Hotel in Buttermere village (NY174169)
Distance: 6.9km (4¼ miles)
Height gain: 93m (305ft)
Type of walk: Tracks and clear lakeside paths; short section of road walking
Refreshments: Croft House Café, Bridge Hotel and Fish Hotel in Buttermere

If you're looking for a really easy walk in some of the most magnificent surroundings in the whole of England, look no further than Buttermere. This little lake, probably one of the most photographed in the Lake District, is ringed by spectacular mountain scenery. With mostly good paths underfoot, you'll have plenty of time to enjoy the views. Starting from the village of Buttermere, your eye will inevitably be drawn to Fleetwith Pike and its impressive ridge at the south-eastern end of the lake, but take some time to enjoy the views across to Goat Crag towering above the northern shore. And, once you've turned the corner and started walking back from Gatesgarth Farm, the impressive High Stile range to the south-west dominates the scene.

TAKE THE PUBLIC BRIDLEWAY which runs to the left of the Fish Hotel – signposted Buttermere Lake and Scale Bridge. Passing through several gates and ignoring a path signposted to Scale Bridge on the right along the way, keep to this wide track as it winds its way to the lakeshore. After going through the gate that gives access

Short Walks

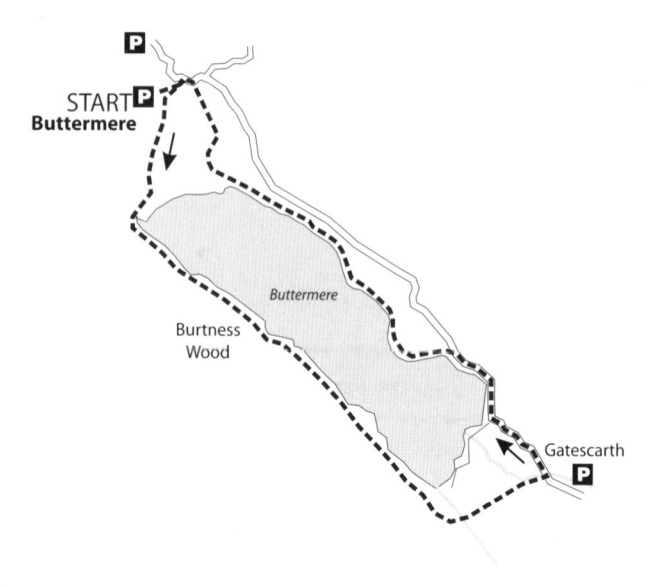

to the lake, turn right, soon crossing the lake outlet stream via a bridge. Ignoring a rocky path heading up to the right, the path swings left to cross a small bridge soon followed by a gate.

Turn left along the lakeshore path, ignoring a path heading steeply uphill through the trees to your right. Bear left at a fork in the track, keeping to the lakeshore path. Just after a brief gap in the trees to the left, where you will see a small shingle beach, you reach a three-way split in the path. Bear left here. This narrow path hugs the lakeshore for a while before rejoining the track coming in from the right. The path now leaves the woods via a small gate. Soon after crossing a footbridge over Comb Beck, the tumultuous stream pouring down from the mountains above, ignore the path heading uphill.

IN THE LAKE DISTRICT

Before long, you reach a signposted kissing-gate. The path to the right leads up to the pass at Scarth Gap and, eventually, Haystacks, the craggy little mountain you can see just ahead and to the right. It's tempting, but leave Haystacks for another day (see Walk 23). Go through the gate. The wide track leads to Gatesgarth Farm. Turn left along the road. Soon after you reach the lakeshore again, take the gravel path off to your left.

The path winds its way along the lake, back towards the village. Soon after crossing a small bridge below Hassness House, the large, white building perched on the high ground up to your right, you go through a gate. Ignore the path off to the right here and keep going along the increasingly narrow lakeshore path. You soon go through a short, dark tunnel that has been cut into the rock.

Hassness House was originally built for the Wright family – of coal-tar soap fame. It is now used as a base for Ramblers walking holidays. The tunnel here was built by employees of an earlier owner of the Hassness Estate, the 19th-century Manchester mill owner George Benson, who wanted to be able to walk around the lake without straying too far from its shore.

When you reach the NW end of the lake, go through a small gate, beyond which the route forks. Keep straight ahead, soon going through a gate and up the side of some exposed rock. At the top of the next section of fenced path, turn left. The track continues between the buildings of Wilkinsyke Farm – and past the ice-cream shop – to reach the road just below the tiny church. Turn left and you will see the Bridge and the Fish hotels on your left in a few metres.

The **Fish Hotel** was home, 200 years ago, to Mary Robinson, the 'Beauty of Buttermere' made famous in Melvyn Bragg's novel *The Maid of Buttermere*. She first became a celebrity in 1792 when Captain Budworth wrote about her in his *Fortnight's Ramble to the Lakes,* saying: "Her hair was thick and long, of a dark brown and, though unadorned with ringlets, did not seem to want them; her face was a fine oval, with full eyes and lips as red as vermilion..."

Consequently, she received many noteworthy visitors, including Wordsworth. In 1802, an apparently prosperous tourist arrived in Keswick – Colonel the Honourable Alexander Augustus Hope, MP for Linlithgow and brother of Lord Hopetoun. He seduced Mary and married her at nearby Lorton.

When the newspapers reported the wedding, Scottish readers pointed out that the real Colonel Hope was in Vienna. Mary had married an imposter – John Hatfield, a linen draper's traveller who was wanted for forgery and bigamy. He had married two women previously, abandoning them when their money started running low. He had also been signing documents in the guise of an MP.

He was arrested in Cumbria but escaped, eventually reaching Wales where he was caught. Although Mary refused to testify against him, he was tried in Carlisle and was hanged in 1803 for forgery. Mary later married a Caldbeck farmer. ◆

IN THE LAKE DISTRICT

20
RANNERDALE KNOTTS

Start/Finish: Lake District National Park car park (Pay and Display) behind the Bridge Hotel in Buttermere village (NY174169)
Distance: 8.2km (5 miles)
Height gain: 382m (1,245ft)
Type of walk: Farm paths; woodland trails; good paths on open fellside and in valley; mostly grassy ridge
Refreshments: Croft House Café, Bridge Hotel and Fish Hotel in Buttermere

Rannerdale Knotts (353m) is a mere whipper-snapper of a fell, sitting at the feet of mighty Grasmoor, just a stone's throw from moody Mellbreak and within shouting distance of the craggy High Stile range. But it can hold its own among these iconic peaks – it hides some surprisingly steep and rocky slopes; its delightful, grassy ridge is a true gem; and the views... well, they're among the best in an area of the Lakes that's full of superlatives.

This walk approaches the fell in a rather roundabout way. It starts from Buttermere, heads out towards Crummock Water and hugs Rannerdale Knotts' southern slopes for superb views across the lake. Dropping back down to lake level, it then climbs steadily through the secluded valley of Rannerdale before finally making for the ridge itself and the walk along to the summit. The return is via an atmospheric wooded ravine.

HEAD TO THE FAR END OF THE CAR PARK, away from the vehicle entrance. Ignoring the two metal gates, go through a kissing-gate over to the right. This gives you access to a beckside path, which you follow downstream.

SHORT WALKS

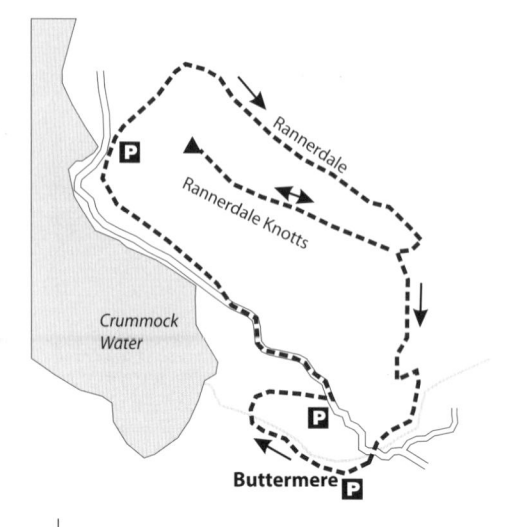

Don't be tempted by the bridge leading into the campsite. Passing through one small gate along the way, keep close to the beck and then cross the stile in the fence on your right.

Once over the footbridge, turn left. The path seems to be making for Crummock Water at first, but then swings right – around the base of a small, wooded knoll. Having passed and ignored a kissing-gate on the left, the path climbs gently through the trees and then drops on to a gravel path, along which you turn left. This quickly swings right – when it does so, keep left, along a grassy path leading to gate. Turn left along the road.

After about 750m, as you draw level with the end of the lake, you will see a small layby on the right. Take the grassy track climbing away from this – signposted Buttermere Hause. This gently rising path cuts a green swathe through the bracken, running almost parallel with the SE shore of Crummock Water and providing superb views of the fells across the water. Keep left at two clear forks, staying on the lower and wider of the routes. Eventually, you reach a point at which you can see down to the northern end of the lake and the path starts to drop. It is quickly joined by another path coming down from the right.

IN THE LAKE DISTRICT

Turn right along the road and then, in a few more metres, right again into a gravel layby. Walking with a wall on the left, you pick up the path around the base of Rannerdale Knotts. Soon after going through a small gate, swing away from the wall and make your way towards the beck. As you approach the water's edge, bear right to head upstream with the beck on your left. Immediately after passing and ignoring a bridge over the beck, go through a small gate in a short section of wall on the right. Continue upstream.

Rannerdale is said to have been the scene of a battle between Norse settlers and the Normans after the 1066 invasion. This local legend is largely based on a fictional account in the book *The Secret Valley*, written by local historian and hotel owner Nicholas Size in 1930. Local folklore states the bluebells that famously carpet the valley floor in May thrive because of the Norman blood split here – or because of the amount of calcium in the soil, a direct result of the bones lying under the ground.

About 450 metres after the path fords a beck, turn right along a narrow path that climbs on to Low Bank ridge. As soon as you reach the top, you get a great view across to Red Pike and the High Stile range. Turn right along the clear, grassy path. This splendid ridge is surprisingly narrow for such a small hill, but never intimidatingly so. You can follow it out as far as you wish, but eventually you will have to retrace your steps.

The highest point at the far western end is marked by a small cairn. When you do finally turn round and head back the way you came, watch carefully for the point at which you first came up on to the ridge. It lies in a small dip. Just before you reach it, bear right along a clear path running almost parallel with the main ridge. Bear right at the next fork and then right again at a path junction. There is a myriad of paths up here, so you need to watch carefully for the relevant turnings. The gradient eases as

Short Walks

you draw level with a fenced coppice over to the right. Bear left at a fork here and, with a beautiful array of mountains ahead, cross straight over one path and down the slope to reach a wall.

Turn left and then, in about 150 metres, go through a small gate in the wall and down some steps to access a beautiful oak woodland beside the beck. The path swings right to head downstream. Turn left at the road and immediately right, beside the Bridge Hotel. Bear right in front of The Fish to re-enter the car park. ◆

The National Trust

The origins of the National Trust, one of the largest conservation charities in Europe, are rooted deeply in the Lake District. In 1875, Canon Hardwicke Rawnsley, vicar of Low Wray Church near Hawkshead, and later Crosthwaite in Keswick, met the social reformer Octavia Hill. Together with lawyer Sir Robert Hunter, they crusaded passionately for a National Trust to be formed to buy and preserve places of natural beauty and historic interest for the nation.

The first building purchased by the trust was Alfriston Clergy House in Sussex, bought for £10 in 1896, but it was in 1902, when the 108-acre Brandelhow estate on the shores of Derwent Water came on the market that the trust set about its most ambitious scheme to date. A brilliant and inspirational speaker, Rawnsley led the campaign to raise funds for the purchase and received nationwide support. The scheme's success was never in doubt with him at the helm, and Princess Louise, daughter of Queen Victoria and a supporter of the National Trust's work, performed Brandelhow's opening ceremony on October 6, 1902. Today, the charity protects a massive 50,000 hectares of land in the Lake District – that's about a quarter of the total area covered by the National Park.

IN THE LAKE DISTRICT

21
AROUND MELLBREAK

Start/Finish: Kirkstile Inn, Loweswater (NY141209)
Distance: 9.3km (5.8 miles)
Total ascent: 279m (915ft)
Type of walk: Valley and lakeside tracks, boggy and rough in places; quiet lanes
Refreshments: Kirkstile Inn, Loweswater

*This walk performs a circuit of **Mellbreak**, the lonely fell that looms darkly over Crummock Water and Loweswater village. It first heads into the lonely valley carved by Mosedale Beck, a wild spot that feels like it's a long way from anywhere. The ascent is so gentle that you'll barely notice you're climbing, and it's on a generally good path – until, that is, you approach the head of the valley. Now, the ground underfoot gets decidedly soggy and the path may be difficult to find. The descent follows the route of Black Beck and Scale Beck, and continues to be rough underfoot until it reaches the delightful Crummock Water lakeshore path. With stunning scenery all around, this takes you almost all the way back to Loweswater.*

FACING MELLBREAK AND WITH YOUR BACK TO THE KIRKSTILE INN, turn right along the lane. Go through the gate in front of a narrow stand of trees and bear right along the wide track.

Follow this bridleway up into the peaceful valley – between Mellbreak on your left and Hen Comb on your right – for about 1.5km (1 mile). You finally leave it just before the fence veers right. Bear left at the faint fork in the path

Short Walks

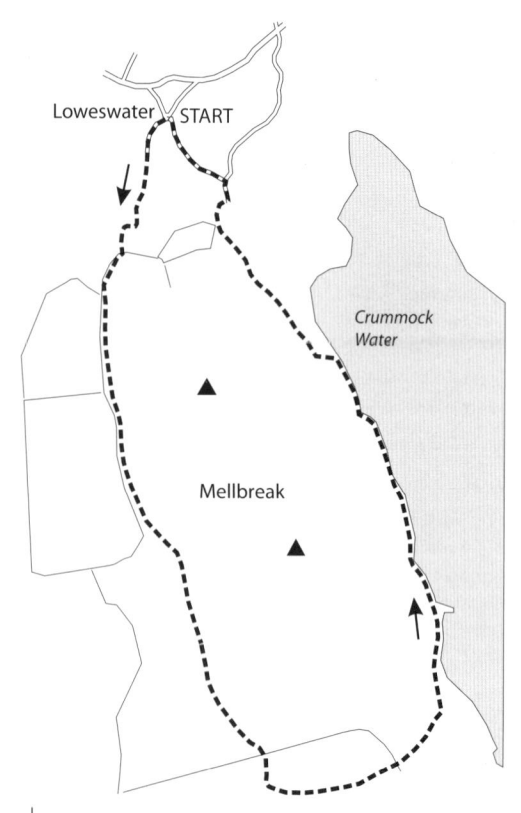

here. Heading slightly uphill at first, the path soon levels off after you pass above the solitary Mosedale Holly Tree.

About 1.3km (¾ mile) after leaving the fence, you will see a narrow, grassy path off to the left. Ignore this. It is followed by a flat-topped rock to the left of the path. Just beyond this, as the path starts to veer left, leave the clear route by bearing right (SE) along a faint path across boggy ground. Eventually, you reach a gate with a stile to the left of it. Cross the stile and head straight down the hill with a fence on your right.

Turn left beside Black Beck. You are on a good path at first, but as you draw level with the tree-cloaked Scale Force over to the right, the route is badly eroded and often boggy as it drops closer to the beck and a dilapidated bridge. Eventually though, the going underfoot improves. Keep following what is left of the beck until you reach a bridge across it, about 400 metres back from the edge of Crummock Water.

Bear left, away from the beck. This path too is frustratingly soggy in places at first, but it soon becomes a thoroughly enjoyable lakeside route.

The mountains on the other side of Crummock Water include Whiteside and, dominating the scene, Grasmoor, while the dark slopes up to your left belong to Mellbreak. The origin of the name Mellbreak is not certain, although it may be a combination of the Welsh word 'moel' – meaning 'bare hill' – and the old Norse word 'brekka'– meaning 'hillslope'. Brekka often refers to a hill whose slopes drop down to the water's edge, as Mellbreak's do.

Approaching the north-western end of the lake, you cross a tumbledown wall. In about 100 metres, having already climbed slightly from the water's edge, bear left along a narrow path. This quickly brings you on to a higher path running almost parallel with the lakeshore path, along which you bear right. Before long, you are walking with a wall on your right. As you approach a group of buildings on the edge of an area of beautiful oak woodland, ignore the small gate down to your right.

Continue to a gate in the trees just above the buildings. Go through this to access a track between drystone walls. Coming out at some dwellings, bear left along the vehicle access lane and then left again at the next junction. At a T-junction, make one final left turn to follow this road back to the pub. ◆

Short Walks

22
Eskdale Moor

Start/Finish: Dalegarth Station in Eskdale (NY173007). There is a pay and display car park here
Distance: 7.7km (4¾ miles)
Total ascent: 264m (865ft)
Type of walk: Good tracks; grassy fell paths, boggy and indistinct in places
Refreshments: Brook House Inn and Boot Inn, both in Boot

Eskdale Moor forms part of a lonely area of relatively low-lying moorland that is shrouded in mystery and legend. Bronze Age people frequented the area in drier times and they have left behind lots of evidence of their existence, including enigmatic stone circles. In more recent times, a corpse road crossed the fell, and this has given rise to stories of phantom horses and magical trees. The walk climbs gently from Eskdale, using the old corpse road before passing close to Burnmoor Tarn and then returning across Eskdale Moor, visiting several stone circles.

LEAVING THE CAR PARK, TURN LEFT and walk along the road until you reach the Brook House Inn. Turn left here to walk into the village. Soon after passing the Boot Inn on your left, keep straight ahead to cross Whillan Beck via a small, humpback bridge – signposted Burnmoor Tarn, Wasdale Head and Miterdale.

There has been a mill on the site here since 1547. The building today has two overshot waterwheels, powering a complex arrangement of wooden hoppers, hoists and millstones.

IN THE LAKE DISTRICT

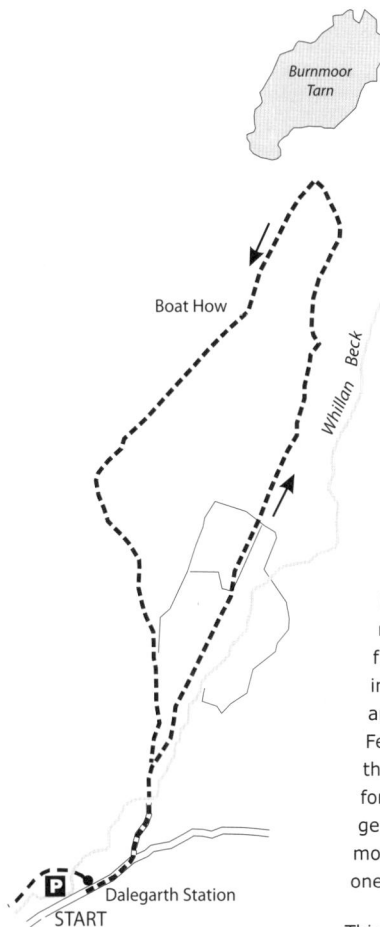

Aim for the rough track heading uphill to the right of a tiny cottage. Beyond the gate, bear right to ascend the bridleway on a wide strip of land between two drystone walls. About 100 metres beyond the gate, turn right through another large wooden gate with a waymarker on it. A stony track gently climbs through the gorse. Beyond the next gate, you pick up the line of a drystone wall on your right and the dome-like top of Sca Fell becomes visible for a short while. After a few more gates, the walk takes on a different nature as the track heads on to open moorland. Hardly half-an-hour from Boot, and you're suddenly in what seems like very wild and remote country. With Sca Fell dominating the view ahead, things are pretty straightforward for now, as you continue the gentle climb. The wide track is mostly stony, although there are one or two damp sections.

This track follows the route of the old 'corpse road'. Before St Olaf's Church at Wasdale Head was licensed for burials, coffins had to be carried on horseback to St Catherine's in Eskdale. This practice continued until 1901.

101

Short Walks

On one stormy winter's day, the horse carrying the coffin of a young local man suddenly took fright and disappeared into the mist near lonely Burnmoor Tarn. The bearers then had the awful task of having to tell the dead man's mother that his body had been lost. The shock proved too much for the old woman and she died soon afterwards. A coffin was again strapped to the back of a horse and the party set off for Eskdale. Again, the group experienced bad weather and, again, the horse bolted. It was never seen again – and nor was the coffin – although it is claimed you can often hear hoofbeats on the moor when the fog descends.

Another local story involves the rowan, a tree said to have restorative properties. As one coffin was being carried from Wasdale to Eskdale, it hit a rowan tree and the dead woman inside was revived.

> About 750 metres beyond the last gate, you will see a small ruin over to the left. The track swings left here and then right again, leaving the true route of the Corpse Road, which continues straight ahead on a slightly lower course. Before long, you crest a rise and you can see across to the mountains of Wasdale, including Kirk Fell. Ignore any narrow paths off until you reach a T-junction just above Burnmoor Lodge. The edge of Burnmoor Tarn is just a couple of hundred metres below now, but this area is crisscrossed with paths so make sure you remember how to get back to this junction if you go exploring.

Burnmoor Lodge was built as a shooting lodge for the lord of the manor, Lord Leconfield, in the 19th century. Today, it is privately owned and is occasionally used by walking groups.

> Turn left here (SW) along a wide, grassy path across Eskdale Moor. Almost 2km (1¼ miles) beyond the junction above Burnmoor Lodge, you reach a fork. Bear right (SW) to head for the first of the stone circles. When you reach the stones, bear left (SE) and then, at the next fork, go left again (ESE) to reach another, larger circle.

It might seem unlikely now, but these lonely, boggy moors were the focus

IN THE LAKE DISTRICT

of much activity in warmer, drier times; and Bronze Age people have left their mark. This is the largest of five circles in the area and consists of 42 stones, only eight of which are still standing. It contains five cairns, which are surrounded by the remains of kerbs. Two of these were excavated in 1827, revealing domes of stones covering cremations, animal bones and antlers.

> Go straight through the middle of this circle and over a small mound. You almost lose the path when you hit a boggy area, but it then swings decisively right (SSE). Don't be distracted by the lesser trails that weave in and out of the 18th-century peat huts. The main track passes below all but one of the stone huts.

Like many Lakeland communities, **Eskdale** once relied heavily on peat as a major source of fuel. The huts on the fellside here, also known as 'peat scales', would have been used by local families as a place for drying and storing peat. The peat would have been cut and left to dry on the moor for a month or so and then brought to the hut by sledge until it was needed in the winter. It was tipped into the hut through the upper door and then shovelled out through the lower one. Peat-cutting continued until the middle of the 20th century.

> Wide and stony beyond the ruins, the track winds its way down to Eskdale. Before long, you are back at the gate above the Whillan Beck bridge. Go through the gate and retrace your steps over the bridge and back to Dalegarth Station.

The **La'al Ratty** (or Ravenglass and Eskdale Railway to give it its proper name) opened in 1875 to carry iron ore from the mine at Boot to the main railway line at Drigg. After the mine's closure in 1882, the line continued to carry passengers until 1908 when it was closed, then reopened, then closed and reopened. For a while in the 1950s it served the quarries at Beckfoot. It was finally bought in 1960 by the Ravenglass and Eskdale Preservation Society. Today, the seven miles of line between Ravenglass and Dalegarth or run by the Wakefield family of Kendal. ◆

Short Walks

23
Haystacks

Start/Finish: Gatesgarth Farm, 3km SE of
Buttermere village (NY194150)
Distance: 7.3km (4½ miles)
Height gain: 545m (1,788ft)
Type of walk: Tracks and fell paths.
The ascent is steep and rocky in places
Refreshments: Croft House Café, Bridge Hotel and Fish Hotel
in nearby Buttermere

*At 598m, **Haystacks** is far from being one of the Lake District's mightiest mountains and yet it has a special quality that makes it a favourite of many walkers. Surrounded by magnificent scenery, it is dwarfed by its neighbours but provides great views across Ennerdale to Pillar and Kirk Fell as well as down to Buttermere. The climb from Scarth Gap to the summit is very steep, almost a scramble at times, so it is probably best not to attempt this walk in snow or ice.*

FROM THE CAR PARK ENTRANCE, cross the road and go through the walkers' gate. Just after crossing a wooden bridge, go through the gate and head steeply uphill to the right of a small group of trees. When you reach the top of this wooded area, bear left with the fence and continue uphill. Almost 1km (½ mile) beyond this left turn, the bridleway passes through a gap in a drystone wall and then appears to fork. Keep left here.

About 400 metres after the path starts levelling off at the pass of Scarth Gap – but before it begins its descent –

IN THE LAKE DISTRICT

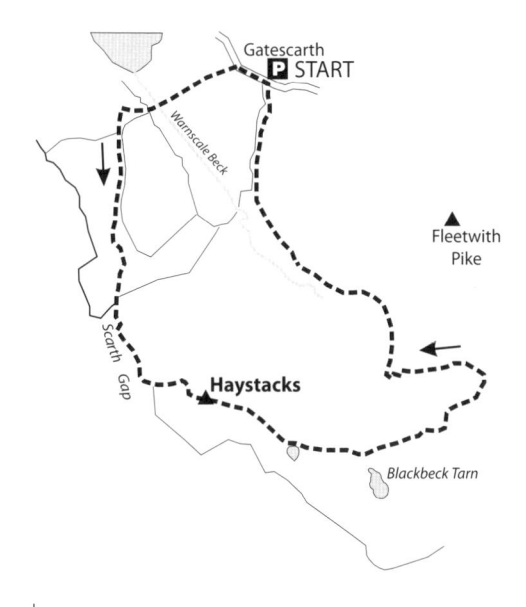

watch for a large cairn to the left. This marks the start of the climb up to Haystacks, a stone staircase that winds its way up the mountainside.

If you're using walking poles, it may be best to put them away at this point as you will probably need your hands on the more difficult sections. After the fairly short but tricky climb, the path levels off and leads to a rocky depression. Head for the large cairn ahead and slightly to your left for some lovely views to the east.

Keep to the right of the small, rocky ridge on a path heading SW. Stay on the rock – do not descend to the tempting grass. The path soon bears left to cross a short section of ridge. Drop down into the gully and follow the path heading south. The path swings left (SE) and winds its way through rocky outcrops, heading NNE for about 300 metres, before swinging round to the SE as it heads towards Innominate Tarn.

Follow the clear path to the left of the tarn – it skirts the water's edge and then swings left (N) to descend and curve

Short Walks

around the head of the valley. After crossing a stream, the path climbs again, swinging right (E) and keeping to the right of a prominent rocky outcrop. You soon join another path, along which you turn left, continuing round the head of the valley. When another path comes in from the right, keep left and start descending. At a fork, keep right and, about 400 metres later, cross a wide stream and bear left along a mostly level path.

About 300 metres after crossing the stream, turn left along a wide path. This descends steeply to the valley floor and around the base of Fleetwith. Turn left at the road, and the car park is about 150 metres ahead on the right.

The white cross visible on Fleetwith Pike's western ridge is a memorial to a young Victorian who died while climbing the fell. The accident happened in 1887 when 18-year-old Fanny Mercer, a servant of a Rugby School master, tripped over her walking pole. ◆

IN THE LAKE DISTRICT

24
CASTLE CRAG

Start/Finish: National Trust car park (Pay and Display)
in Rosthwaite (NY257148)
Distance: 5.2km (3¼ miles)
Height gain: 250m (820ft)
Type of walk: Clear tracks and paths; steep ascent on loose,
potentially slippery slate
Refreshments: Royal Oak Hotel, Scafell Hotel and Flock In tearoom,
all in Rosthwaite

Castle Crag (300m) is the tiny, steep-sided fell that sits in the Jaws of Borrowdale. Small it may be, but it commands an excellent position within the valley, one that has been used by armies for centuries and is now enjoyed by fell-walkers. This walk follows the River Derwent from Rosthwaite and then meanders through the woods at the base of the crag before mounting an assault on the summit fort. It's a short climb, but it's steep – using a loose path through a quarry spoil heap to get to the top. Your reward, however, is the panorama from the top; it's definitely worth every drop of sweat and every extra breath you've panted to get here.

LEAVE THE CAR PARK AND TURN RIGHT along the asphalt lane. After passing Yew Tree Farm – with the Flock-In tearoom on your right – you will find yourself on a farm track between drystone walls. When you reach the River Derwent, follow the track round to the right and then cross via the stone bridge.

Turn right and you will soon come to a choice of gates. Choosing the right-hand one, you have the river for

SHORT WALKS

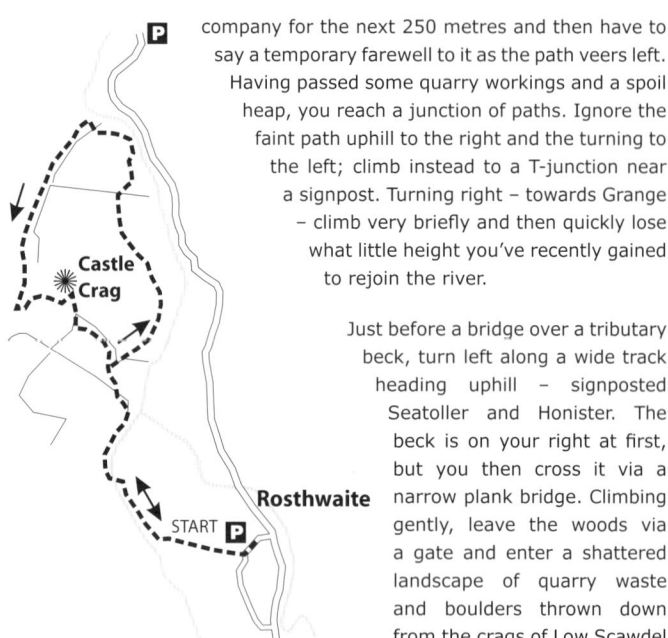

company for the next 250 metres and then have to say a temporary farewell to it as the path veers left. Having passed some quarry workings and a spoil heap, you reach a junction of paths. Ignore the faint path uphill to the right and the turning to the left; climb instead to a T-junction near a signpost. Turning right – towards Grange – climb very briefly and then quickly lose what little height you've recently gained to rejoin the river.

Just before a bridge over a tributary beck, turn left along a wide track heading uphill – signposted Seatoller and Honister. The beck is on your right at first, but you then cross it via a narrow plank bridge. Climbing gently, leave the woods via a gate and enter a shattered landscape of quarry waste and boulders thrown down from the crags of Low Scawdel up to your right. It's not a particularly difficult climb at this stage, but it's worth stopping occasionally to turn around and enjoy the fantastic views of Derwentwater and Skiddaw behind.

About 400 metres beyond the gate, turn left up what is at first a faint, grassy path, but soon becomes a clearer, stony trail that almost doubles back on itself. Go through a gap in a drystone wall, passing a memorial bench to Sir William Hamer on your right. Once over the next ladder stile, followed immediately by a step stile in a fence, turn right to walk with the fence on your right for a short while.

The path soon swings round to the left and climbs to

a cairn at the bottom of some quarry workings. Follow the zig-zag path steeply up through the spoil heap. The slate is relatively stable, but you do need to watch your footing, especially in wet weather. This section of the climb is quickly over and you emerge on to a flat area with superb views down into Borrowdale on your right. There is a path off to the left which explores the cliffs exposed by the quarrymen, but your route continues straight ahead, uphill through some trees and on to the flat, grassy top of Castle Crag. The summit cairn itself is perched on a rocky outcrop that will require some easy scrambling.

Sir William Hamer gave **Castle Crag** to the National Trust in 1920 in memory of his son and 10 other men from Borrowdale who were killed during World War One. There is a war memorial at the summit, and Sir William's wife Agnes erected the memorial seat to her husband on the lower slopes in 1939.

The crag is crowned by the remains of an Iron Age hill fort. Borrowdale, in fact, is the anglicised version of the Norse 'borgar dalr', which means 'valley of the fort'. The Romans also used it, probably taking advantage of its prominent, strategic position within the valley.

The crag has been occupied more recently than that, too. Between the two world wars, two of the crag's caves became the summer home of **Millican Dalton**. Sick of commuting and dissatisfied with his comfortable career in the City, he went back to the county of his birth, Cumberland, when he was in his 30s to offer adventure holidays to would-be climbers in the Lake District. An intelligent and well-educated man, he called himself the Professor of Adventure and offered "camping holidays, mountain rapid shooting, rafting and hair's breadth escapes".

Desperate to get back to nature, Dalton lived at first in a tent at High Lodore in Borrowdale, then in a split-level quarried cave half way up Castle Crag. Despite having a waterfall pouring through his roof, he turned one cave into a living area and one into a bedroom, which he called 'The Attic'.

A strict vegetarian, he grew potatoes on the terrace outside his cave, baked his own bread, ate hazelnuts picked from the woods around his cave and made his own clothes. Dalton loved to pit himself against the elements. He climbed trees in winter to keep fit for climbing and, on his 50th ascent of Napes Needle, is said to have lit a fire on the airy summit and made a pot of coffee.

Normally, he would spend winters in the forest hut that he built for himself in Buckinghamshire, but during the London Blitz of 1940/41, he braved snow, ice and sub-zero temperatures to remain all winter on Castle Crag. Sadly, he didn't get to end his days in his home county; he died in hospital in Amersham after contracting pneumonia in 1947 – at the age of 79.

> Once you've soaked up the views, particularly that stunning outlook north towards Skiddaw and Derwentwater, retrace your steps to the bottom of the zigzagging path through the spoil heap. Now bear left and, as the path forks near the drystone wall, turn left to cross a ladder stile. (There are two ladder stiles in this wall; you want the higher of the two.) The grassy path on the other side heads downhill (SE). Once through a small gate in a wall, the path becomes steep and loose in places.

If you are lucky, you may hear the sound of the Borrowdale cuckoo during the spring and early summer. Legend has it that the good people of this valley once built a wall across their beautiful dale to keep the cuckoo in so that spring would last forever. When the bird inevitably flew over the barricade, one of the dalesmen cried: "By gow! If we'd nobbut laid another line o' stanes atop, we'd a copped 'im!" This is supposedly why the dialect word for cuckoo – 'gowk' – also means 'fool'.

> Cross a stile beside a gate and turn right along the track. Once through the next gate, turn left to cross the humpback bridge over the River Derwent and then retrace your steps to the car park in Rosthwaite. ◆

IN THE LAKE DISTRICT

25

ABOVE THIRLMERE

Start/Finish: Station Coppice car park (Pay and Display) on western side of A591 (NY315170)
Distance: 6.4km (4 miles)
Height gain: 291m (955ft)
Type of walk: Woodland trails; farm path; track along the base of the fells
Refreshments: King's Head Hotel at Thirlspot

*There is plenty of variety on this relatively short walk. It starts by following a permissive path along the eastern shore of **Thirlmere** where you will see plenty of birdlife and, if you're lucky, red squirrels. The second half is a complete contrast. After climbing a short distance, it crosses the open fellside, using a stony but level path through the bracken, providing good views of the reservoir and passing beneath attractive waterfalls.*

FROM THE BOTTOM OF THE STEPS hidden away on the western side of the car park, go through the left-hand gate along the permissive path – towards the dam and Legburthwaite. The muddy path heads downhill, soon with a fenced gorge on the left. As you approach the reservoir, follow the clear path as it swings right. The first of several United Utilities waymarkers appears as you draw level with Fisher Gill and the rather forbidding Middlesteads Gill on the other side of the water. Make sure you follow these waymarkers to keep to the lakeshore path.

United Utilities has followed a policy of thinning the forests beside Thirlmere over the last couple of years, so the views – for both walkers

Short Walks

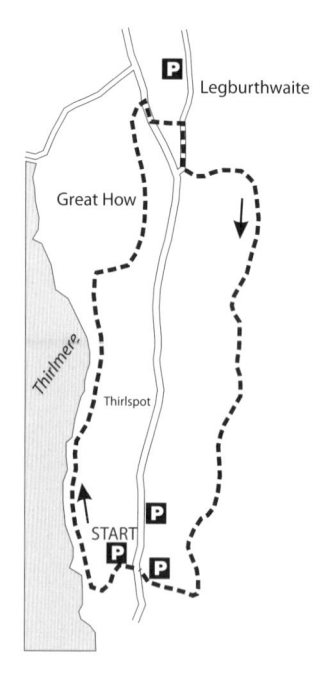

and drivers using the A591 – are much better than they used to be. You'll often be able to see Thirlmere as you head north. It started life as two small, natural lakes which were joined together and enlarged in the late 19th century to form a reservoir. Victorian engineers devised a system, still in use today, which allows water to flow by gravity, without any pumps, all the way from the reservoir to Manchester, nearly 100 miles away. The water flows at a speed of almost 4mph and takes just over a day to reach the city.

It was in 1874 that Manchester Corporation advisers realised that the city's ever increasing demand for water, then averaging 18 million gallons per day, would soon exhaust the supply. They first recommended sourcing water from Ullswater, but it was later decided to create Thirlmere. Despite being stalled by the Thirlmere Defence Association, the project eventually received Royal Assent in 1879 and Manchester was granted the right to extract 25 gallons of water per head per day. The first water to arrive in Manchester from Thirlmere was marked with an official ceremony on October 13, 1894.

You soon go through a kissing-gate and then, as you cross the first of several small footbridges, you can see Dale Head Hotel up to the right. Beyond the next gate, you pick up a surfaced track climbing gently. Swinging away from the water, your views of the opposite shore are now replaced by your first glimpse of the fells to the east. The path winds its way gradually uphill towards the foot of Great How.

IN THE LAKE DISTRICT

Keep your eyes peeled for red squirrels in this area. Part of the 4,800-hectare Thirlmere estate became the country's first red squirrel refuge in 2002. It is hoped that careful management of the woodland here will help protect the reds. Rope bridges have been installed for the squirrels' safety and special food hoppers provided.

When you reach a crossing of footpaths at a signpost, turn right – towards Legburthwaite. With a fence on the right, the track soon heads downhill to reach a junction with another track. Turn left, as indicated by the waymarkers.

Carefully cross straight over the busy road and turn right along the grass verge. After about 100 metres, watch out for steps on the left leading down the embankment. Descend these and climb the stile. Cross the field, keeping close to the wall on your right. If you look to your left now, you will be able to see Blencathra's southern arêtes just appearing in the gap between High Rigg and the craggy western slopes of Clough Head. Leave the field via a gate and then turn right along the road. Just after passing some white houses, turn left up Stanah Lane. You will pass the entrance to a small Caravan Club site on your right and then, as the lane swings sharp left, cross the ladder stile straight ahead.

A muddy path climbs gently to a gate, beyond which you cross the leat and then continue to another gate. The path swings right to cross Sty Beck, climbs slightly and then forks. Bear right here – towards Swirls car park. The path quickly levels off and you keep fairly close to the wall on your right until you reach a fork above the buildings at Fisher Place. As indicated by the waymarker, bear left, away from the wall. Cross the gated footbridge over Fisherplace Gill, which contains a series of pools and impressive waterfalls tumbling down from the high fells above. The path soon picks up the line of the wall again on the right. Just after fording a small beck, bear left at a junction of paths – towards Swirls car park and Helvellyn.

Eventually, you reach the junction with the path heading up on to Helvellyn via Browncove Crags. Turn right here, heading downhill. The path crosses a small bridge, goes through a couple of gates and then crosses another bridge to enter the Swirls car park. Just before you leave the car park, watch for a narrow path to the right of the access road. This will drop you back on to the A591 opposite the Station Coppice car park. Be careful as you recross this busy road. ◆

Alpaca

You might catch sight of some unusual livestock in the fields around Thirlspot: in among the sheep are a few alpaca. Their origins go back to ancient Andean civilizations where they were kept at altitudes of between 3,500m and 5,000m, but these distinctive creatures are becoming increasingly popular in Cumbria too. They are largely bred for their coats, which produce a warm fibre used in knitted and woven garments such as jumpers, hats, gloves and scarves. But they serve another purpose too, and one that makes them ideal for Cumbrian farmers – they act as sheep guards. Gelded males, in particular, are good at fending off predators such as foxes and dogs. Some farmers also claim the animals make sure that lambs don't stray too far from their mothers, rounding up youngsters who wander from the flock.

Sometimes mistaken for llamas, alpacas are considerably smaller than their camelid cousins and, unlike llamas, were bred specifically for their fibre not as beasts of burden.

IN THE LAKE DISTRICT

26

ALCOCK TARN

Start/Finish: The parish church of St Oswald's in Grasmere village (NY306225)
Distance: 5.3km (3¼ miles)
Height gain: 312m (1,022ft)
Type of walk: Ascent of fell uses a good path, but route down is less clear; some road walking
Refreshments: Choice of cafés, pubs and restaurants in Grasmere

*Pretty little **Alcock Tarn** lies in a grassy bowl high above Grasmere, on the western slopes of Heron Pike. Despite it involving a fairly steep climb from the village – followed by an equally steep descent – it remains a popular destination for those looking for a short, fairly straightforward walk up from the valley.*

The views on the ascent, particularly up towards Dunmail Raise, are magnificent and provide a good excuse for frequent rests. The return journey takes on quite a different character as you head down into wilder terrain at the foot of Great Rigg. Here, it is not the distant views that draw the attention, but the perfect, u-shaped valley formed by Greenhead Gill.

THE WALK STARTS FROM ST OSWALD'S CHURCH in Grasmere village, where William Wordsworth and various members of his family are buried. From the church porch, walk out on to the road and turn left, heading out of Grasmere. At a small roundabout, turn right on to the A591 and then immediately left on to a minor road.

You soon pass **Dove Cottage**, where Wordsworth and his sister Dorothy

Short Walks

lived from 1799 until 1808. Built in the 1600s, it was originally an inn called the Dove and Olive Branch. The building has been open to visitors since 1899 and still houses much of the Wordsworths' original furniture.

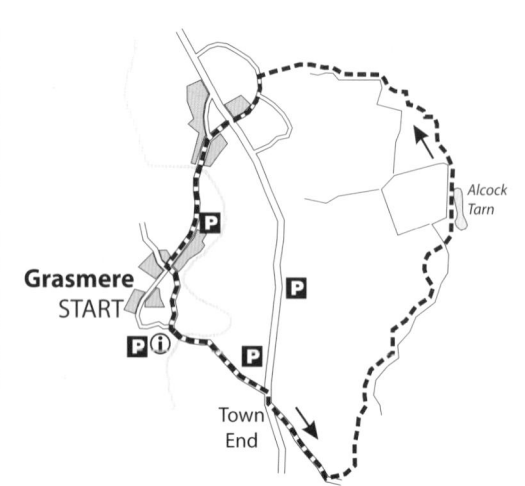

The Dove Cottage years were an extremely good period in Wordsworth's life. He was writing some of his best work and, in 1802, he married his and Dorothy's life-long friend Mary Hutchinson. At about the same time, Sir James Lowther died and his long-standing debt to the Wordsworths was finally paid off, meaning that William and Dorothy were finally in a more comfortable financial situation.

The Wordsworths received many guests at Dove Cottage, including Sir Walter Scott, Robert Southey and, their most frequent visitor, the poet Coleridge. After the Wordsworths moved out, Dove Cottage became the home of the poet's young friend, Thomas de Quincey, although he soon upset the family by making alterations to their beloved garden. He actually lived there for 22 years, much longer than the Wordsworths. As well as the many fascinating Wordsworthian artefacts on show in Dove Cottage, there is also a set of scales which is said to have been used by de Quincey to weigh his opium.

As you continue to climb gently uphill on the quiet, asphalted lane, the next interesting feature you see is the Coffin Stone, a large rock just to

IN THE LAKE DISTRICT

the left of the road. This road used to be part of a 'corpse road'. Before St Mary's Church in Ambleside was consecrated, coffins had to be transported along this route from Ambleside to St Oswald's Church in Grasmere for interment. The Coffin Stone (also known as the Resting Stone) was used to support the coffin while the bearers rested.

> Ignore one turning on the left and then, as the lane swings right, turn left to head more steeply uphill – signposted Alcock Tarn. At the next right-hand bend, turn left on to a track – towards Alcock Tarn. Having ignored a narrow path heading steeply uphill beside a wall, go through a large metal gate into the National Trust woodland at Brackenfell. The track continues to climb, moderately for now, and then goes through a second metal gate. There is a bench on the left here should you need a rest – or simply want to savour the views over Grasmere.
>
> Ignoring a permitted path off to the left, follow the yellow waymarked route round to the right. This snakes its way up the fell, eventually passing through a gate on to the National Trust land surrounding Alcock Tarn. It climbs to a stream, crosses it and then becomes narrower as the zigzags tighten. After the zigzags, the path swings left and passes through a gap in a drystone wall to reach Alcock Tarn. The path keeps to the left of the tarn, soon following the line of a drystone wall. Go through a small metal gate and skirt a boggy area on your right.
>
> Just after a large cairn, the path splits. Be careful here because it may at first look like the main path goes left, but you actually need to take the less obvious branch, heading to the right of a rocky area and crossing a boggy patch via some stones. The steep path follows a series of zigzags and eventually drops to Greenhead Gill. When you reach the beck, turn left to follow it downstream.
>
> You soon reach a small, wooden bridge. Cross this and go

Short Walks

through the gate on your left. You are now on a surfaced lane heading downhill. Turn left at a T-junction and drop to the Swan Hotel on the A591. Carefully cross the road, turn right and immediately left towards Grasmere. When you reach the village proper, turn left after a row of shops. At the next T-junction, turn left to return to the church. ♦

William Wordsworth

The name William Wordsworth is inextricably linked with Cumbria. He was born in Cockermouth on April 7, 1770, the son of a lawyer who worked as an agent for the wealthy Lowther family. He spent most of his childhood in Cockermouth and Penrith, his mother's home town. From 1779 until 1787, he attended Hawkshead Grammar School, and it was here that he was encouraged to write poetry.

After graduating from Cambridge, he travelled in Europe and spent some time living in Somerset with his sister Dorothy, but, with the 18th century drawing to a close, he returned to his beloved Lake District, setting up home in Grasmere and, later, Rydal. He married his childhood friend, Mary Hutchinson, in 1802, the couple eventually having five children.

The beauty of the landscape in which he lived, together with his love of walking, had a profound influence on Wordsworth's life and his poetry. Many of the 70,000 lines of verse that he wrote focus on the natural world.

IN THE LAKE DISTRICT

27

DOCK TARN AND GREAT CRAG

Start/Finish: Stonethwaite in Borrowdale (NY262137)
Distance: 7.7km (4¾ miles)
Height gain: 445m (1,460ft)
Type of walk: Woodland; steep ascent; some pathless, open fell which may be boggy in places
Refreshments: Langstrath Inn, Stonethwaite

*Surrounded by purple heather and grey crags, **Dock Tarn** is a lovely, secluded spot high above busy Borrowdale, more akin to the Scottish Highlands than the Lake District fells. This walk approaches it via Lingy End, a steep route up through glorious oak woods. It also visits Great Crag to the NW of the tarn, a fell which, despite its modest height of 452m, provides some great views of Borrowdale and Skiddaw.*

An added bonus in the second half of the walk is the beautifully situated hamlet of Watendlath, and an opportunity for a tea break in the little café here before descending to Stonethwaite via straightforward tracks and paths.

FACING THE PHONE BOX IN STONETHWAITE, turn left towards Grasmere and Greenup Edge. The wide track soon crosses Stonethwaite Beck, beyond which you turn right. In about 250 metres, you will see a small sheepfold up to your left. A few metres beyond this, cross the gap in the low, stone wall on your left. A grassy path climbs beside a small beck and then crosses it. As soon as the path reaches a wall, cross it via the awkward stile, beyond which you begin climbing through oak woodland.

Short Walks

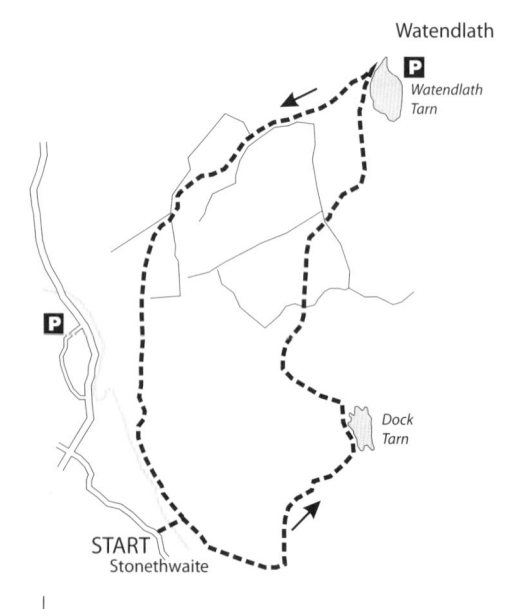

Depending on what time of year you are here, the path may be partly obscured by leaves, but there are cairns to guide you. It quickly leads to a wooden stile, beyond which the climb gets a lot steeper. You're on a mostly pitched path, apart from one or two short sections where the bedrock is exposed. When you break free of the trees, the path continues to climb. As you climb the next stile, take a moment to turn round and enjoy the great views down lonely Langstrath. It looks pretty bleak from up here. The gradient eases slightly as you make your way up to Dock Tarn alongside rushing becks and in between knolls thickly cloaked in heather.

As you catch your first sight of the tarn, bear right to follow the path around the western edge of the tarn. Continue beyond the northern end of the tarn for about 70 metres, ignoring any paths off to the right. Now turn left on a faint, grassy path heading W. This skirts the edge of a boggy depression and, at the far end of this, you swing right. At the top of this short slope, watch carefully for a faint path heading uphill through the heather to the left (NNW). Take this to reach a rocky, heathery knoll with a steep path ascending its eastern slope. Having climbed

IN THE LAKE DISTRICT

> this, follow the obvious path swinging right (N) to the cairn-topped summit of Great Crag.

There's a fine **panorama** of fells from here, including Skiddaw, Helvellyn and Bow Fell. In particular, the verdant floor of upper Borrowdale, backed by Great Gable, Lingmell and Scafell Pike, draws the eye to the SW.

> The path continues in roughly the same direction beyond the summit. A branch heads off to the left to climb to a slightly lower summit, also topped by a cairn, but our route continues along the main path. This descends rough ground and eventually drops to a clear, stony track along which you turn left. Just after the next kissing-gate, ford the beck and then continue along the obvious path. This consists of an almost solid line of stepping stones across the wetland. They end at a grassy junction of paths near a signpost. Turn right here towards Watendlath Tarn.
>
> The path leads down through a kissing-gate and then beside a beck. After fording the beck, it becomes indistinct, but if you keep close to the wall on your left, you will soon pick it up again. Eventually, you reach a junction of paths beside the tarn. The route turns left here, but Watendlath, to the right, is worth a short detour, especially when the tearoom is open.

The pretty, unspoilt hamlet of **Watendlath** is hidden high above Borrowdale in one of the area's hanging valleys. 'Hanging' above the level of the glaciated valley floor, it was gouged out by a tributary to the main glacier, and so didn't erode as deeply.

The hamlet, which didn't get mains electricity until 1978, was the setting for Hugh Walpole's 1931 novel *Judith Paris*. It was the second of four novels belonging to the Herries Chronicle. Set in Keswick, Borrowdale, Watendlath, Uldale and Ireby, these books told the story of the Herries family from the 18th century to the depression of the 1930s. Foldhead Farm is generally thought to be the model for Rogue Herries Farm, the home of the eponymous heroine.

Short Walks

Hugh Walpole was born in New Zealand in 1884, but lived in Cumbria from 1924 until his death in 1941. He made his home on the lower slopes of Cat Bells on the western side of Derwent Water. Brackenburn, his "little paradise on Cat Bells", received many literary visitors including JB Priestley, Arthur Ransome and WH Auden.

> Turning left at the junction – towards Rosthwaite – you climb for a short while and then begin the descent to Borrowdale. Don't be tempted by the kissing-gate in the wall on the right and then, at the next junction of paths, ignore the large gate on the right, which would take you down to Rosthwaite. Simply continue towards Stonethwaite. At a T-junction, turn left along the wide, valley track. Having followed Stonethwaite Beck for about 700 metres, turn right to recross the beck and return to Stonethwaite. ◆

IN THE LAKE DISTRICT

28

TAYLORGILL FORCE AND STYHEAD TARN

Start/Finish: Seathwaite in Borrowdale (NY235123). The roadside parking leading to Seathwaite fills up early, so walkers may need to park in the National Trust pay and display car park in Seatoller, which is 2km (1¼ miles) from the start of the walk.
Distance: 6.1km (3¾ miles)
Height gain: 325m (1,066ft)
Type of walk: Valley path; steep ascent involving easy scrambling; descent uses good tracks
Refreshments: Yew Tree, Seatoller

You might look at the distance and the total ascent on this walk and think you were in for a fairly easy half-day, but you'd be mistaken. The path up the north-western side of Taylorgill, the side which provides the best views of the waterfall, is very steep and rocky. You will need to use your hands as you clamber up along the base of the crags, and some walkers may be unnerved by the steep drops into the rocky valley below. Consult your nerves – and be honest about your head for heights – before setting out.

Having said that, if you enjoy a bit of easy scrambling, this is the best and most exciting way of seeing Taylorgill Force, the dramatic waterfall that plunges more than 40 metres through this pine-clad ravine. Beyond the gill itself, the route continues upstream, through the wild valley between Great Gable and Seathwaite Fell, to reach Styhead Tarn, sitting at the foot of some of Lakeland's biggest mountains. After that tricky ascent,

SHORT WALKS

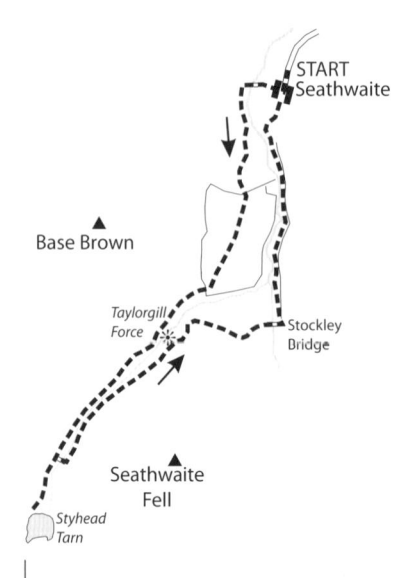

the return is then a walk in the park! A steady stroll back down the other side of the valley on a good, well-used path takes you all the way back into Seathwaite.

WALK SOUTH AND INTO THE FARMYARD. Go through a gated gap in the barn on the right to access a track. (Signs on the wall indicate that this is also the way to the campsite.) Cross the footbridge over the beck and then turn left through the gate. You are now on a beckside path, which manages to be both rocky and soggy at the same time. Things become fractionally easier underfoot as you pass through a gate in a deer fence and gently climb the lower slopes of Base Brown. Beyond a ladder stile, the path, indistinct in places, continues its gradual ascent, now making a beeline for the craggy, northern slopes of Seathwaite Fell to the south.

When you finally enter Taylorgill, the path swings sharp right. This is where things begin to get more difficult. As you scramble up the first rocky section to a gate occupying a narrow ledge at the base of the crag, keep close to the rock wall on your right. There is a path closer to the edge, but this is very loose – put a foot wrong and you'll end up at the bottom of the gill far below. There is quite a bit more scrambling to do beyond the gate, but it is divided into relatively short pitches. You'll have plenty of opportunity to stop, get your breath back and admire Taylorgill Force in between climbs. As you begin

IN THE LAKE DISTRICT

to draw level with the waterfall, the going briefly becomes a little easier and more staircase-like. The next awkward section, which involves a short drop that may leave some walkers feeling rather exposed, can be avoided by using a faint path that briefly heads up to the right. You then need to ease your way around some rocks jutting out over the chasm, but after this, things become much easier.

Cross a rocky gully and continue uphill with a wall/fence on your left, soon passing the top of the waterfall. The valley begins to widen now as you follow Styhead Gill upstream. Things aren't all plain-sailing though; even here, the path is badly eroded in places and there are one or two loose sections with steep drops down to the left. Eventually, the gradient eases and you pass a footbridge. Ignore this, although you will return to this point after visiting Styhead Tarn. For now though, continue following the beck, and in another 300 metres, you reach the tarn.

Right at the very base of some of the Lake District's mightiest fells, this makes a good spot to sit and ponder the possibility of venturing further into these dramatic mountains. Great Gable can be easily climbed via the path up Aaron Slack to the NW; immediately S of the tarn is craggy Great End, accessed by walkers from the Esk Hause path, climbing SE; the bridleway you have been following since the bridge would take you over Styhead Pass and down into magnificent Wasdale; while the path heading SW is the Corridor Route, one of the main routes on to Scafell Pike.

Once you've rested, retrace your steps to the bridge, cross the beck and follow the clear path downstream on the eastern side of the valley.

The bridleway drops to the valley bottom where it goes through a gate, crosses Stockley Bridge and then swings left to follow Grains Gill downstream. Before long, you are back in Seathwaite where the walk started.

Seathwaite is famous for being the wettest inhabited place in the country. The rain gauge that measures rainfall here is slightly further up the valley near Sprinkling Tarn. The biggest deluge ever recorded during one 24-hour period in the whole of the UK was at Sprinkling Tarn in November 2009 – a massive 314mm, or more than one foot of rain. This resulted in serious flooding downstream in Keswick, Cockermouth and Workington and the death of PC Bill Barker when Workington's Northside Bridge collapsed.

In total, more than 2,200 properties were flooded, three road bridges destroyed and a further 20 road bridges closed. In addition, 253 of the Lake District's 1,200 footbridges were damaged or destroyed and 85 paths suffered as a result of the downpour. Cumbria's path network suffered an estimated £3.2 million worth of damage. ◆

Graphite

As you walk back into Seathwaite at the end of the walk, you will see spoil heaps up on the slopes to the west. These belong to the now disused 'wad' mines. Wad is the local name for plumbago, more commonly known as graphite.

The discovery of graphite, early in the 16th century, gave rise, several hundred years later, to Keswick's famous pencil industry. According to local legend, it all started with a violent storm in Borrowdale, which led to trees being uprooted and the discovery of an unknown black material underneath. Shepherds then began using the mysterious substance to mark their sheep, creating the world's first pencils.

Pencil-making remained a cottage industry for a long time – until 1832, in fact, when the country's first pencil factory was established at Braithwaite, near Keswick. At the end of the 19th century, following a fire at its Braithwaite premises, the Cumberland Pencil Company moved into Keswick itself, where a pencil museum was also established. The museum is still there, but the factory recently moved to Cumbria's west coast.

IN THE LAKE DISTRICT

29

LINGMOOR FELL AND SIDE PIKE

Start/Finish: National Trust's Blea Tarn car park (NY295043)
Distance: 7.4km (4½ miles)
Height gain: 450m (1,476ft)
Type of walk: Woodland paths; indistinct, sometimes rough paths on summit ridge; narrow rock squeeze; valley paths and tracks, damp in places
Refreshments: Brambles coffee shop and Wainwrights' Inn, Chapel Stile; Britannia Inn, Elterwater

*With illustrious neighbours such as the Langdale Pikes, Wetherlam and Crinkle Crags towering over it, this has to be one of the best low-level fell walks in the whole of Cumbria – a sort of Lake District in miniature. At 469m and 344m respectively, **Lingmoor Fell** and **Side Pike** are really only small bumps on the Lakeland landscape, but don't be fooled into thinking you are in for an easy time. The walk on to Lingmoor Fell from Little Langdale is fairly straightforward, but there are some exciting moments on the ridge with surprisingly steep sections of rocky descent and even a narrow rock squeeze that some people may find difficult. At the end of the walk, you drop to beautiful Blea Tarn.*

TURN LEFT OUT OF THE CAR PARK, cross the cattle grid and walk along the road for just over 1km (½ mile).

This area is one of the last strongholds of the **juniper** bush. The Lake District used to be covered in huge forests of the stuff, but much of it has gone now. Its decline has been particularly marked over the last 50 years.

127

Short Walks

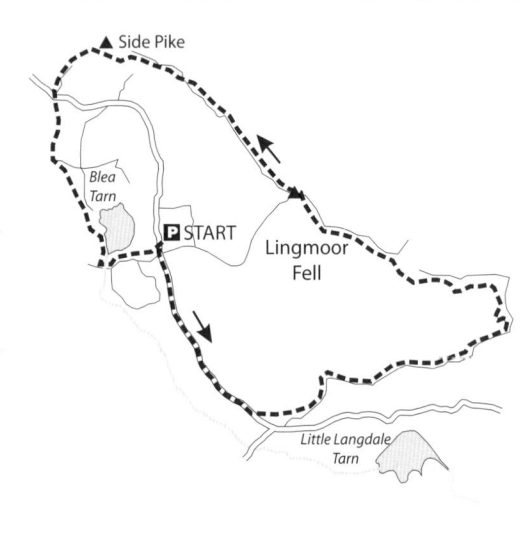

Many old juniper bushes are not being naturally replaced owing to shading from other plants and grazing pressures from rabbits and livestock. Attempts are now being made in some parts of Cumbria to replant areas with young juniper bushes. In Longsleddale a few years ago, climbers were brought in to plant the conifers on inaccessible crags where they would be safe from sheep. The berries provide an important food source for birds and animals such as field mice, squirrels and badgers.

In the 17th century, the herbalist Nicholas Culpepper recommended the berries as a treatment for asthma and sciatica. He also claimed they could speed childbirth. If you get a chance, squeeze one of the berries and then sniff it. There's no mistaking which spirit this is used to flavour – gin.

Just before the road reaches the valley bottom, turn left up a grassy track, which has a low wooden barrier across it. You climb briefly and soon have a wall on your left as you make your way across some damp ground. As the wall starts to climb away from the path, you will see another coming up from the right. This will now act as your guide for about 1.2km (¾ mile). Just after a kissing-gate, you ford a small beck. Don't be tempted by the rock shute heading straight up the slope here; instead, turn

IN THE LAKE DISTRICT

right immediately, clambering over some rocks to gain a narrow, beckside route. As the beck quickly swings away, rejoin the line of the wall. This pleasant path, which skirts the base of Lingmoor Fell, is mostly easy underfoot, but it does become a little rougher after passing the buildings at High Bield, where it briefly climbs more steeply.

Keep to the path nearest the wall and you eventually reach a gate. Don't go through this; instead, turn left. It's a fairly steep climb on to the ridge, but it's all on grass. When you reach the top and begin to swing W at first, then more NW, you will find there are several paths to choose from. Generally speaking, you should keep as close as possible to the wall on the ridge proper. It's an undulating route and has a few twists and false summits along it, but the wall will eventually guide you to the cairn on Brown How, the highest point on Lingmoor Fell. You may lose sight of the wall on occasions. On one such occasion, you crest a rise to get your first breathtaking view of Crinkle Crags and Bow Fell. From here, the ridge path drops and then climbs and then dips slightly again. The wall now swings sharp right and becomes a fence as it starts to climb more steeply. As it does so, the path briefly swings away from the wall. In a few metres, bear right along a narrow, stony path climbing steeply. You soon regain the fence, which you will cross via a stile to reach the summit cairn.

Continue downhill with the dilapidated wall/fence on your immediate left. There is a long drop to Side Pike and the path is steep and rocky. When you reach a fence corner, turn left to descend steeply with the fence and then wall on your left. The wall continues to be your faithful companion guiding you down some rough ground. With the worst of the descent behind you, cross a stile and then continue downhill with the wall on your right. This path will take you all the way to the base of Side Pike's formidable buttresses straight ahead.

Cross a stile in a fence and then continue up towards the steep rock face. Only as you reach the base of the crag does the path finally swing left to find a route around the southern side of Side Pike. It clings tightly to a ledge and then squeezes its way through a narrow gap between the rocks. The path soon swings right and climbs. When the Langdales reappear, the path splits. Bear right if you want to climb to the summit of Side Pike, but the main route bears left. Follow the wall on your right until the path goes through a gap in it.

With the ground suddenly dropping away steeply, the route ahead is unclear. Basically, you need to pick up a path, cairned in places, that negotiates several shallow rocky ledges to descend in a mostly WSW direction. As you approach the base of the fell, make your way back over to the wall on the left and then climb the ladder stile to reach a minor road.

Cross straight over and then, a few metres back from the road, go through the gate in the wall on the left to access a constructed path. Before long, you have Blea Tarn on your left. Cross the bridge at the southern end of the tarn and swing left to return to the car park. ◆

30

Seat Sandal

Start/Finish: Layby on the eastern side of the A591, about 2km (1¼ miles) S of the Pass of Dunmail Raise (NY335096). [NOTE: This is *not* the car park with the AA box just south of the pass.]
Distance: 8.2km (5 miles)
Height gain: 697m (2,286ft)
Type of walk: Valley track; steep, but mostly grassy ridge path; open fell; some damp sections on descent
Refreshments: Choice of cafés, pubs and restaurants in nearby Grasmere

Seat Sandal (736m), from the old Norse meaning 'Sandulf's summer pasture', is a lonely top that sits by itself, overshadowed by its more famous neighbours, Helvellyn and Fairfield. The only people who come up here are peak baggers and fell-walkers seeking a quiet alternative to the more well-trodden fells. This route ascends via a faint path up the steep, but grassy southern ridge, and then drops down to Grisedale Tarn before descending via Little Tongue. If you enjoy stunning all-round views, and you want to keep them to yourself, this is a great walk. The biggest drawback is that it's so short.

LEAVE THE LAYBY AND WALK DOWN THE MAIN ROAD – towards Grasmere. Just as you draw level with a minor road turning on your right, turn left along a rough track – signposted Patterdale. The track passes to the left of a cottage called Tongue Ghyll and then passes through a gate to begin climbing alongside a noisy beck. The slopes

SHORT WALKS

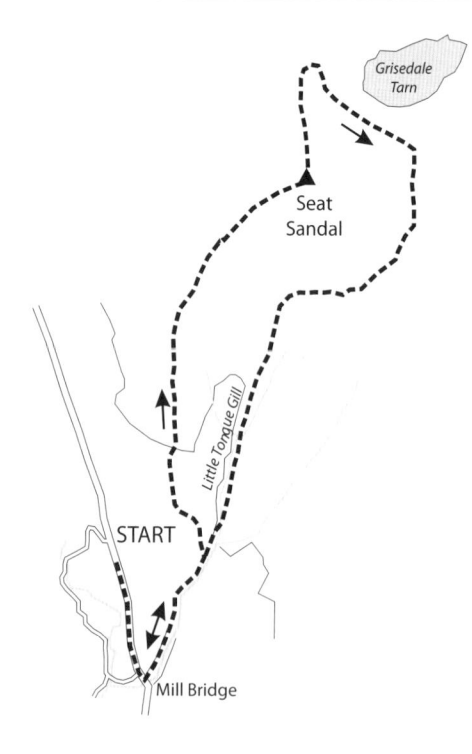

of Seat Sandal are visible straight ahead.

About 700 metres after leaving the road, watch for a tiny building on the other side of the gill. Soon after this, go through the small wooden gate on your left to enter a tiny enclosure. Head for the narrow gap in the wall corner up to your right. Once through this, turn left to walk with the wall on your left. Go through the gate in the wall corner and then turn right. You are now on a faint path through the bracken, climbing beside the wall on your right. Before long, this swings away from the wall to climb to a wooden gate. Go through this and head up the reasonably clear ridge path. You climb alongside the wall at first, but it isn't long before you lose this guide.

After the next small gate, you are on the open fell. The path continues through the bracken and some rock outcrops. Although the view straight ahead is not particularly inspiring, if you take your time and turn around occasionally as you climb, more and more peaks will slowly join the magnificent panorama of mountains

IN THE LAKE DISTRICT

to the left and behind you. Steel Fell, Crinkle Crags, Pike O'Blisco and the Coniston fells are visible early on. Later, Bow Fell, the Scafell range and Great Gable appear too. As the ridge broadens, you get your first tantalising glimpses of the scenery to the north, including the fells above Coledale. Keep heading straight up the slope. As you approach the summit area, the path weaves about a bit; it is very faint now, so make sure you don't lose it as it twists and turns. Eventually, as Helvellyn, Skiddaw and, on a clear day, the Scottish hills come into view, you reach the first of the summit cairns. Continue across the grassy top to the cairn marking the highest point. You can now look down Grisedale to Ullswater, with the slopes of St Sunday Crag looming above the valley. The line of blue hills in the distance is the Pennines.

Cross the tumbledown wall just beyond the cairn and turn left to descend with the wall on your immediate left. As you lose height, Grisedale Tarn appears in the bowl on your right. At the bottom of the slope, you reach a dip with some redundant fenceposts in it. Turn right and then, in about 20 metres, turn right again along a path that contours the hillside, with the tarn below to your left.

Dunmail Raise, which marks the old boundary between Cumberland and Westmorland, is named after Dunmail, the last Celtic king of Cumbria. He was defeated by Edmund I, the Saxon king of England, in a battle at the pass in 945AD. There are several versions of the story about what happened to Dunmail. Some say that, following his defeat, he fled to Rome. Another legend says that Edmund personally killed Dunmail on the battlefield. Dunmail's warriors, so the story goes, retrieved the crown from their dying leader's head and threw it into Grisedale Tarn to prevent the Saxon king from flaunting it.

When the path forks, keep right and make your way towards the wall up ahead. On reaching the wall at a junction of paths at Grisedale Hause, go through the gap in it and begin descending into the next valley.

About 500 metres beyond Grisedale Hause, having leapt across a beck, turn right along a narrower path contouring the fellside. The ground is a bit damp, but the views and solitude make it all worthwhile. The path becomes indistinct as it crosses an especially boggy area and goes over to grass. Be careful here, because it swings slightly left (SSE) to head more steeply downhill. The path gets a lot clearer again after fording a beck.

Before long, you reach a path junction at a confluence of becks. Turn right to cross Little Tongue Gill. Go through a gap in a wall followed by a gate, and you should soon recognise this track as the one you followed at the start of the walk. Now retrace your steps, remembering to turn right when you reach the road. ◆

Other titles by

QUESTA PUBLISHING LIMITED

LAKE DISTRICT
WALKS WITH CHILDREN
Buttermere and the Vale of Lorton
Around Coniston
Keswick and the Newlands Valley
Ullswater
Around Kendal
Around Windermere
South Lakeland

EASY RAMBLES
Around Keswick and Borrowdale
Around Ambleside and Grasmere
Around Eskdale
Around Wasdale
Around Ennerdale & Calder Valley
Around Dunnerdale
Around Coniston and Hawkshead
Around Patterdale and Ullswater
Around the Langdale Valleys

YORKSHIRE DALES
WALKS WITH CHILDREN
Wharfedale
Swaledale
Wensleydale
Malham and Airedale
Ribblesdale

PEAK DISTRICT
WALKS WITH CHILDREN
Dark Peak

PENNINES
SHORT WALKS
Eden Valley and North Pennines

All QUESTA titles are available by post from
27 Camwood, Clayton-le-Woods, BAMBER BRIDGE, Lancashire PR5 8LA;
by FAX to 0705 349 1743, or
EMAIL to sales@questapublishing.co.uk

www.questapublishing.co.uk

IN THE LAKE DISTRICT